CHRIS

MW01145131

BOOK OF SHARED SPIRITUALITY

SECOND EDITION

Christ the Victor and *World Impact Wichita* are ministries of World Impact, Inc.

World Impact Wichita
3701 E 13th St N
Wichita, KS 67208

Scripture quotations marked ESV are from The Holy Bible, English Standard
Version® (ESV®), copyright © 2001 by Crossway, a publishing ministry of Good
News Publishers. All rights reserved.

All resources marked TUMI are from The Urban Ministry Institute. Used by
Permission. All rights reserved. www.tumi.org

TABLE OF CONTENTS

5 ~ Appendices 131

1

INTRODUCTION

BISHOP GREETING

Greetings in the name of our Victorious Savior!

It is my distinct privilege to welcome you to the second edition of our Christ the Victor *Book of Shared Spirituality*. It is our hope that this updated book continues to be an even more effective guide as we form our spiritual life together under the headship of Christ as CTV Church Movement.

After having given myself fully to this idea of submitting to a shared spirituality with like-minded brothers and sisters in Christ since our movement began in 2008, I believe immersing ourselves in the concepts of this book will be the most powerful statement we can make as a movement seeking to bring Christ to our hurting world. Truly, the life of Christ lived out in the power of the Spirit by the unified and bonded-together church, will have the single greatest impact to those who live under the reign of the evil one.

The purpose of this book is very simple – to make us more like Christ *together*. Following after Christ on the narrow path is not easy, but neither is it complicated. It is available to all who call upon Christ as Lord, and it is our greatest privilege as his bride to ready ourselves for the great wedding day to come. In many ways, sharing an ancient spirituality focused on Christ and handed down to us from the Apostles is like keeping the drum beat of God's great kingdom from eternity past to eternity future.

Brothers and sisters, ready yourselves for battle by steadying yourselves with this ancient rhythm of living the life of Christ *together*. Let us agree with the Apostle Paul as we fight for the honor of our King, "for me to live is Christ, to die is gain."

Rev. Daren Busenitz

CERTIFICATION

This *Book of Shared Spirituality* truly reflects and embodies the beliefs and practices of Christ the Victor Church (CTV). It is a reliable source for CTV bishops, pastors, deacons, leaders, and congregants to understand and participate in our Christ-centered shared spirituality.

This is the second edition of the *Book of Shared Spirituality* (2014). In the course of time, it may be that new editions of this book will become necessary. In such a case the head bishop and the Custodian of CTV Documents and Resources, in consultation with bishops and pastors, will evaluate potential changes and updates, and produce a new edition. Until such a time as a new edition is produced, the content of this edition is to be followed.

In Christ Our Victor,

Ryan Carter
CTV Custodian of Documents and Resources
Kingdomtide, 2014

HOW TO USE THIS BOOK

The CTV *Book of Shared Spirituality* (*BOSS*) is a resource that helps your church make the Christ-centered journey together through the year both as the gathered body in worship and as the dispersed body in the world. This book gives both the raw material and the blueprint for powerful shared life.

Pastoral Use

For the busy pastor, this book can serve as a basic guide for organizing church life and services. The Sunday lectionary and church year information (seasonal names, themes, colors, etc.) are provided. You can plan your service weeks and months ahead. It also provides common themes, prayers, and Bible readings that you can easily reference as your congregation tracks through the year together.

If your whole church uses the *BOSS* together, it can provide a collective spiritual well from which everyone may draw. Sermons, prayers, services, devotions, small groups, discipleship, and children's lessons can all be focused on the same ideas and texts. This sort of continuity empowers you as a pastor to guide your whole congregation as one. Allow this book to unify and integrate the different elements of your church. The church year is a powerful pastoral tool that you can use to your advantage. The seasons and celebrations direct your collective attention to Christ. The lectionary allows you to chart a course that will meet the needs of your congregation while still maintaining a balanced, Christ-centered focus on the whole counsel of God. Go through the seasons and choose series of texts from the lectionary. Develop your own themes and ideas from these texts in line with the seasonal focus of the church year.

This book can also provide safeguards for you as a pastor. All too often, it falls solely on pastors to lead the church, plan the services, decide what to preach, and dictate curriculum for programs. In this environment, it is easy for your personality and preferences to become the rule of the church rather than the person of Christ and the kingdom of God. Following this book can aid you in staying on a Christ-centered track. It can lead you and your church in the ancient and powerful way of Christian faith and worship.

Congregational Use

The *BOSS* is a great resource to put in the hands of your people. It can serve as the centerpiece of a congregational shared spirituality. It keeps everyone on track with the story of Christ told through the church year. This provides a strong core of common identity and practice that can unify and strengthen your congregation.

Allow this book to guide your congregational life and shape your various meetings. Make the life and work of Christ the central reality of your community life. Participate with Jesus in the movements and events of his incarnation. Allow the seasonal themes to set the mood and approach of your times together. Read and meditate upon the same Scriptures and give the Holy Spirit a path to work in the whole body as one. There is great power in an entire congregation sharing tangible things in common. This book provides meaningful substance that your church body can share.

Family/Small Group and Individual Use

In a world where many place high value on the new and unique, this book can serve as a guide to the steady, well-trodden paths of personal spirituality. This book contains nothing inventive or new. It is a guide to the way of spirituality that has marked most Christians throughout the ages. Through the use of this book, each of your families or small groups can find meaning in the context of the church as a whole. Each individual can share alone-together disciplines not only with the local congregation, but also with the universal body of Christ in all places at all times.

Both family/small group spirituality and personal spirituality are meant to fit into the context of congregational spirituality. Focus on the themes, pray the prayers, read the texts, and meditate on the passages provided here. Your connection with one another through these practices will give the Holy Spirit avenues by which he can speak to you through one another. He will give insight and guidance to each family/small group and person individually. That insight and guidance when shared in community will be significant and relevant because of a common focus.

Our Prayer

Our prayer is that in the consistent use of the *BOSS*, your congregation, families or small groups, and you personally will find the power of a shared spirituality centered on Christ. Use this book as a tool to focus your spiritual attention on Jesus Christ our Lord. Trust in faith that he will meet you in his word, in your community, in relationships, in conversations, in worship, and in prayer. We pray also that this book will empower you as a congregation, as families and small groups, and as individuals to have a deep, shared spirituality. Through that common commitment, we pray God expands his kingdom by reproducing churches in the city!

2

CHRIST THE VICTOR CHURCH: A QUICK GUIDE

THE WAR WE ENTER

The Need We Face: We are called to the *darkest, hardest,* and *poorest* places of our cities

The Dominion of Darkness

The tragic circumstances of many urban communities cannot be explained by simply pointing to bad choices and personal sin. Too often, the devil has been allowed free reign in our cities and the disastrous effects of his oppression are clear.

The Path of Hard Resistance

High rates of crime and dysfunction communicate that urban neighborhoods are dangerous, hard places. The result is that the dominion of darkness goes largely unchallenged. Sin and evil are allowed to take deep root in hearts, lives, homes, families and whole communities.

The Crushing Weight of Poverty

Poverty is one of the most daunting and overwhelming problems in our world. The chronic lack of resources and opportunities creates real hopelessness and powerlessness among the urban poor. Poverty becomes a crushing weight that traps people and offers only tiny windows of escape.

The Call We Embrace: We seek an urban *church planting movement.*

Only the powerful presence of God's kingdom through his church will do for the needs of the city.

Christ the Victor was born out of World Impact's vibrant missionary zeal to see the urban poor come to Christ. Our passion to reach the city for Christ thrived and grew despite the impossible and complicated circumstances found in so many poor neighborhoods.

We have always believed that the church was the answer for the city and yet it was difficult for the church in the inner city to survive, grow, and multiply. However, as we learned about church planting movements in foreign missions (the rapid multiplication of churches planting churches), we asked ourselves 'What if the Lord would touch our inner-cities with revival and multiply churches among the urban poor?'

Of course, we recognize that church planting movements are God's own work of revival, not the result of skill or technique. We cannot follow a recipe to make it happen. We can only be faithful to do what God is calling us to do.

Christ the Victor Church is crafted for a church planting movement should God choose to bring revival. In everything we have intentionally sought to be reproducible so that it is possible to quickly train and release leaders, and to empower churches to multiply in the city.

Retrieving the Great Tradition: What is worth reproducing everywhere?

The Ancient Faith

Jude wrote his epistle to challenge the church "to contend for the faith that was once for all delivered to the saints" (Jude 3). Christianity neither began with us, nor is it fundamentally defined by us. We are in the position of receiving and embodying a faith that was defined in the ancient past. When we enter the body of Christ, we step into a river that has been flowing from the days of the prophets, Christ, and the apostles. We have only to embrace and contend for the ancient faith in an ever- changing world.

An Urban Movement

As we seek an urban church planting movement, we see tremendous value in centering churches on what has been believed and practiced everywhere, always, by all Christians. The ability to reproduce quickly means that CTV churches cannot be required to reinvent church with every new church plant. Certain beliefs, practices, and protocols need to be standardized. But as soon as we start talking about standardizing things, we must answer a second question, 'What is worth reproducing everywhere?'

Christ the Victor, therefore, intentionally seeks to retrieve the Great Tradition in our theology, worship, spirituality, and mission. "The Great Tradition represents that central core of Christian belief and practice derived from the Scriptures that runs between the time of Christ and the middle of the fifth century. In a formative way, this Tradition articulates the church's faith and practice, its joyful, faithful response to the truth of God's sovereign work of grace in the world" (Don Davis, *Sacred Roots*, TUMI, 2010, p.74).

OUR BATTLE CRY

Christ the Victor Churches *live* the victory of Jesus, *seek* the advance of his kingdom in the city, and *stand* on the ancient Christian faith.

CTV *lives* the spectacular story of the victory of God's kingdom through Jesus Christ.

The story of the Bible is the victory of God's kingdom through Jesus Christ.

The eternal God our Lord is the creator and ruler of all things. In pride, Satan rebelled against the Lord's reign and ignited a cosmic war. Human beings, created in God's own image, joined the rebellion by obeying Satan, the ancient serpent. God's world was plunged into darkness and subjected to sin and death. Yet, in his infinite mercy, the Lord promised to send a Savior to crush evil and redeem his creation. God sent his own Son, Jesus, down from heaven to invade the dark realm of Satan. Through Christ's life, death, resurrection, and ascension, the devil is defeated. When Jesus sat down at the right hand of the Father, he sent his Holy Spirit to empower us, the church, as we declare his victory in all the earth, and call everyone everywhere to flee the oppressive reign of the devil and to enter the blessed kingdom of his Son. Very soon, the Lord will completely conquer Satan and all demonic activity, and destroy sin and death, and he will establish his eternal kingdom. As followers of Christ, we are privileged to faithfully represent Christ as the Victor and coming King who destroys the works of the devil. The fight is on!

CTV *seeks* a movement of churches that aggressively pursues the advance of God's kingdom by the power of the Holy Spirit.

By the will and power of the Lord, Christ the Victor will be an unstoppable global movement of CTV churches, which declare and demonstrate the victory of the kingdom of God through Jesus Christ. We will experience warm fellowship and shared spirituality in vibrant churches of common identity and practice that confess and embody the richness and depth of the ancient Christian faith. We will empower the least in the world's eyes to be great in the kingdom of God. We will prayerfully and aggressively seek the advance of God's kingdom, stopping at nothing to win the hardest, darkest and poorest places in our cities for Christ.

CTV *stands* on the ancient Christian faith as it has been believed and practiced everywhere, always, by all.

❖ A shared spirituality centered on Christ and celebrated through the church year

❖ A historic theology anchored in Scripture and summarized by the Nicene Creed

❖ A focused mission committed to reproduction that results in indigenous church planting movements

WE BELIEVE THE TRUTH: OUR THEOLOGY

The story of God in Christ confessed through the Nicene Creed is the summary of our faith. We make this great confession as a way of declaring the truth of the story of Scripture.

The Nicene Creed (AD 325, 381)[1]

We believe in one God, the Father Almighty, maker of heaven and earth and of all things visible and invisible.

We believe in one Lord Jesus Christ, the only begotten Son of God, begotten of the Father before all ages, God from God, Light from Light, true God from true God, begotten not created, of the same essence as the Father, through whom all things were made.

Who for us men and for our salvation came down from heaven and was incarnate by the Holy Spirit and the Virgin Mary and became human. Who for us too, was crucified under Pontius Pilate, suffered and was buried. The third day He rose again according to the Scriptures, ascended into heaven and is seated at the right hand of the Father. He will come again in glory to judge the living and the dead, and His kingdom will have no end.

We believe in the Holy Spirit, the Lord and life-giver, who proceeds from the Father and the Son, who together with the Father and the Son is worshiped and glorified, who spoke by the prophets.

We believe in one holy, catholic[2], and apostolic church.

We acknowledge one baptism for the forgiveness of sin, and we look for the resurrection of the dead and the life of the age to come.

Amen.

---

[1] See also *The Nicene Creed with Biblical Support and Explanation* (Appendix 2, pp. 134–38).

[2] For more on this term see *The Term 'Catholic'* (Appendix 3, pp. 139–41).

WE WORSHIP THE KING: OUR WORSHIP AND LITURGY

In worship the church retells and reenacts the story of God. We retell the great story and remember the actions and promises of the Lord. Then we engage in a dramatic reenactment of the story as we participate in the body and blood of the Lord.

Worship: Responding to God

The God who is accomplishing the victory of his kingdom through his own Son is worthy of all praise (Rev 5.12). Worship is a response to the infinite person and gracious works of Almighty God (Ps 107.2). Continual perfect praise is always offered before the Lord in heaven (Rev 4.8). In worship we join with the voices of the heavenly beings to declare his worth and his glory because of who he is and what he does.

Liturgy: The Form of Worship

Following the ancient church traditions about worship, the Liturgy of the CTV Sacred Service is organized into two large movements, the Word and the Table. Each of these movements is broken down into three parts so that there are six major blocks to our liturgy. The graphic below illustrates these blocks.[3]

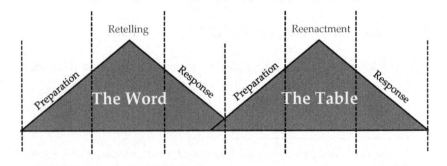

---

[3] See also the CTV *Liturgy of the Sacred Service* (Appendix 4, pp.142–49).

Baptism and Communion: A Theology of the Sacraments

A Bath and A Meal

You are part of a great family living together in the household of God (Eph 2.19). As adopted sons and daughters of the Almighty, the church is your new home. Like any good parent, the Lord bathes and feeds his children.

Baptism and communion are the two sacraments commanded by Christ in Scripture, the bath and the meal (Matt 28.19; 1 Cor 11.23–26). In these outward physical signs, the amazing inward spiritual grace of God fills you with life. The sacraments are not magic, but rather they present God's grace to you in a material way. Through your faith, the Holy Spirit applies the cleansing and sustaining grace of God to your life.

Baptism – Washed by the Spirit[4]

Baptism is your incorporation into the visible body of Christ. It is a public pledge to renounce sin and evil, to die to yourself, and to live under the lordship of Jesus Christ as a part of his church.

The outward visible sign of baptism is your going down into water in the name of the Father, the Son, and the Holy Spirit and coming up to walk in the new life.

The inward spiritual grace of baptism is that by grace through faith you are united with Christ's death and burial, and raised to a new life in the Holy Spirit. You are incorporated into the Body of Christ by adoption into the family of God, and ordained into the royal priesthood that worships and serves the Lord. The victory of Christ over sin and death is applied to you, and you enlist as part of his spiritual army.

---

[4] See also the CTV *Liturgy of Baptism* (Appendix 5, pp. 150–54).

Communion – Fed by Christ

Communion is the memorial of your redemption in Christ, our Passover — that is in his life, death, resurrection, ascension, session[5] and the anticipation of his impending return. In communion the sacrifice of Christ is made present to the church. This is the heart and summit of the church's life and the central act of your ongoing spiritual life.

The outward visible sign of communion is the bread and the fruit of the vine given and received in the baptized community of the church.

The inward spiritual grace of communion is that, in a manner that is mysterious, the body and blood of the Lord Jesus are made present to you in the elements of communion. In the sacrament the Lord applies to you the grace of ongoing forgiveness, of strengthening your union with Christ and with the family of God. He nourishes you with spiritual food to sustain you through these days of battle and struggle. He also offers you a foretaste of the heavenly banquet of the age to come, and calls you to hope in the day when his victory is made complete.

---

[5] Christ's seating at the right hand of the Father.

WE FOLLOW THE NAZARENE: OUR SHARED SPIRITUALITY AND PASTORAL LEADERSHIP

The story of God in Christ lived through the church year provides the structure for our worship and spirituality. Year after year the church walks the journey of Jesus' incarnation. Services, themes, images, readings, prayers, and spiritual disciplines all join together to enrich this journey. We do this together under the watchful care of pastoral leaders.

Shared Spirituality – Knowing God Together

The victory of God's kingdom through Jesus Christ invites the church into a unique and intimate relationship with God. Spirituality is, in essence, your side of the relationship. Shared spirituality is the practice of relating to God as a community first, and then secondly as individuals. Christ the Victor Church is convinced that community spirituality is logically prior to and more fundamental to the Christian life than individual personal spirituality.

Embodying the Story of God in Christ through Discipleship

As you follow Christ and pattern your life after him, the Spirit of God transforms you to become like him (Rom 8.29). There are three major ways that discipleship plays out in the church.

A disciple lives the baptized life.

Through discipleship the church helps you understand and live the reality of your baptism by renouncing sin and evil, dying to yourself, and living under the lordship of Jesus as a part of his church.

A disciple walks the path of the church year.

The church year serves as the structure for your ongoing discipleship. As the church takes the yearly journey through Christ's story, his life becomes the pattern of our shared life.

A disciple joins in the shared life of the church.

Discipleship happens in the church under the care of a pastor (Heb 13.7, 17). As the baptized community walks the journey of the church year, the family of God nurtures the young as they grow. Older, more mature believers walk the way with younger believers so they can show them how to follow Christ.

Under the Watchful Care of Pastoral Leaders

God has given gifted men and women to the church as pastoral leaders who can instruct, equip, care for, and discipline the flock of God. Church leadership is *rooted* in the victory of the kingdom of God through Jesus Christ as told in Scripture. Leaders participate with God in his work with the church. By his own authority, the Lord calls leaders into his service. As Christ's ambassadors, church leaders serve as his *representatives* carrying out his desires in the body. Within the bounds of representation, church leaders take *responsibility* for leading the church. Ultimately, church leaders must be about empowering new leaders for *reproduction*.

WE SERVE THE LORD: OUR WITNESS

The story of God in Christ is continued in our mission. We seek the advance of God's kingdom reign through reproducing disciples and churches.

Continuing the Story

When you became a part of the church, you entered the plotline of God's unfolding drama. God is working to bring about his own eternal purpose to establish his kingdom by defeating evil and bringing grace and forgiveness through Jesus Christ. Our ministry and mission are a participation in the person and work of the Triune God. This great mission of God has been worked out in and through his people. We continue the story.

By the Power of the Holy Spirit

The victory of God's kingdom through Jesus Christ is a tangible and present reality that you can know and live today. You can truly experience his victory in your life, your church, and your community. We desire to experience Christ's victory over sin, death, and evil by seeking the Spirit's manifest presence and power in our midst! Only God working powerfully through his Spirit could possibly accomplish the vision of a church planting movement among the urban poor.

Especially Among the Poor

Christ the Victor is called to the darkest, hardest, and poorest places of our cities. We are deeply convinced that the Holy Spirit can and will empower the lowest and the least in the world's eyes to be great in the kingdom of God. We expect great things from the urban poor as laborers and ambassadors for Christ. We trust that God will empower new generations of leaders and release them into urban harvest!

WHAT DOES IT MEAN TO ENLIST WITH CTV?

To join with CTV is to enlist in an army of men and women dedicated completely to the service of our Lord. Together we enter this war, raise a common banner, and seek Jesus' victory in the cities of our world.

Entering the War

If you are going to enter the war with us, you must…

- ❖ **Detest the Enemy** – We fight a strong and deadly enemy who wreaks havoc in our cities, destroys our communities, and enslaves people in darkness. You must learn to hate what is evil (Rom 12.9), and join Christ in destroying the works of the devil (1 John 3.8).

- ❖ **Declare the Victor** – Enlisting with CTV means living the victory of Christ. Jesus of Nazareth has defeated sin, death, and the devil. He is victorious and he reigns. It is only in him that we have the boldness to face the dominion of darkness, and it is only in his victory that our cities can have hope.

- ❖ **Determine Your Allegiance** – While the battle is cosmic, it is fought through the local church. You must decide if the Lord is calling you to enter this great war with Christ the Victor Church.

Raising the Banner

Raising our common banner means that you...

- ❖ **Root Yourself in CTV Deeply** – No one fights without training and equipment. Take the time to learn essential identity and practices of CTV.

- ❖ **Represent CTV Courageously** – Stand firm on the essentials of the faith while proclaiming and demonstrating Christ's victory in the city.

- ❖ **Reproduce CTV Faithfully** – Pass on the faith you have heard and believed to faithful disciples who will, in turn, be able to train others!

Seeking the Victory

Seeking the victory of Jesus with us means that you...

- ❖ **Pledge Yourself to the Mission** – By the will and power of the Lord, we will be an unstoppable global movement of CTV churches, which declare and demonstrate the victory of the kingdom of God through Jesus Christ. Enlisting with us means pursuing this mission with focus and dedication.

- ❖ **Place Yourself Under Authority** – Submitting to authority is an essential part of enlisting with CTV. We are far stronger and more effective if we fight this battle together under the guidance of pastoral leaders.

- ❖ **Persevere to the End** – Paul declared, "I die every day" (1 Cor 15.31). The battle is hard. Nothing about ministering the gospel in the city is easy. In the face of hardship, confusion, fear or danger, we keep fighting and persevere to the end knowing that our labor is not in vain (1 Cor 15.58)!

3

DAILY DEVOTIONS

A MODEL FOR PERSONAL DEVOTIONS

1. Opening Prayer – Say the following prayer:

> Eternal God our Lord you are the creator and ruler of all things.
> In pride, Satan rebelled against you and ignited a cosmic war.
> Though we were created in your own image, we joined the
> rebellion by obeying Satan, the ancient serpent. In our sin we
> were separated from you and fell under the power of the evil
> one. Your creation was plunged into darkness and subjected to
> death.
> Lord, in your infinite mercy, you promised to send a Savior to
> crush evil and redeem a people for yourself. In the fullness of
> time, you sent your own Son, Jesus, down from heaven to invade
> the dark realm of Satan. Through Christ's life, death,
> resurrection, and ascension, you defeated the devil and opened
> the kingdom of heaven to all believers.
> Very soon, you will send your Son again to this world and he
> will completely conquer Satan and all demonic activity. He will
> destroy sin and death and establish your eternal kingdom.

OR Use this prayer:

> You are God: we praise you; You are the Lord: we acclaim you;
> You are the eternal Father: all creation worships you.
> To you all angels, all the powers of heaven,
> Cherubim and Seraphim, sing in endless praise:
> Holy, holy, holy Lord, God of power and might,
> heaven and earth are full of your glory.
> The glorious company of apostles praise you.
> The noble fellowship of prophets praise you.
> The white robed army of martyrs praise you.
> Throughout the world the holy Church acclaims you;
> Father, of majesty unbounded, your true and only Son, worthy
> of all worship, and the Holy Spirit, advocate and guide.

You, Christ, are the King of glory, the eternal Son of the Father. When you became man to set us free you did not shun the Virgin's womb. You overcame the sting of death and opened the kingdom of heaven to all believers. You are seated at God's right hand in glory.

We believe that you will come and be our judge.

Come then, Lord, and help your people, bought with the price of your own blood, and bring us with your saints to glory everlasting.

2. Daily Bible Reading (see The Daily Readings, pp. 34–45)

3. Reflection – Prayer, Journaling, Silence, etc.

4. Church Year Weekly Prayer (see Church Year Weekly Guide, pp. 65–129)

5. Personal Prayer – Praises, Petitions, Supplications

6. Read Passage for Memorization/Meditation (see Church Year Weekly Guide, pp. 65–129)

7. The Lord's Prayer

Our Father in heaven,
Hallowed be your name;
Your kingdom come, Your will be done on earth as it is in heaven;
Give us this day our daily bread;
And forgive us our debts, as we also have forgiven our debtors;
And lead us not into temptation, but deliver us from evil;
For yours is the kingdom and the power and the glory forever.
Amen

A MODEL FOR FAMILY DEVOTIONS

1. Opening Prayer – Say one of the follow prayers:

   Eternal God our Lord you are the creator and ruler of all things. In pride, Satan rebelled against you and ignited a cosmic war. Though we were created in your own image, we joined the rebellion by obeying Satan, the ancient serpent. In our sin we were separated from you and fell under the power of the evil one. Your creation was plunged into darkness and subjected to death.

   Lord, in your infinite mercy, you promised to send a Savior to crush evil and redeem a people for yourself. In the fullness of time, you sent your own Son, Jesus, down from heaven to invade the dark realm of Satan. Through Christ's life, death, resurrection, and ascension, you defeated the devil and opened the kingdom of heaven to all believers.

   Very soon, you will send your Son again to this world and he will completely conquer Satan and all demonic activity. He will destroy sin and death and establish your eternal kingdom.

OR

   You are God: we praise you; You are the Lord: we acclaim you;
   You are the eternal Father: all creation worships you.
   To you all angels, all the powers of heaven,
   Cherubim and Seraphim, sing in endless praise:
   Holy, holy, holy Lord, God of power and might,
   heaven and earth are full of your glory.
   The glorious company of apostles praise you.
   The noble fellowship of prophets praise you.
   The white robed army of martyrs praise you.
   Throughout the world the holy Church acclaims you;
   Father, of majesty unbounded, your true and only Son, worthy
   of all worship, and the Holy Spirit, advocate and guide.

You, Christ, are the King of glory, the eternal Son of the Father. When you became man to set us free you did not shun the Virgin's womb. You overcame the sting of death and opened the kingdom of heaven to all believers. You are seated at God's right hand in glory.

We believe that you will come and be our judge.

Come then, Lord, and help your people, bought with the price of your own blood, and bring us with your saints to glory everlasting.

2. Daily Bible Reading – Portion or all of the Daily Reading (pp. 34–45), or Passage for Memorization/ Meditation (see Church Year Weekly Guide, pp. 65–129)

3. Conversation about the Passage

4. Church Year Weekly Prayer (see Church Year Weekly Guide, pp. 65–129)

5. Family Prayer – Praises, Petitions, Supplications

6. Recite the Nicene Creed

    We believe in one God, the Father Almighty, maker of heaven and earth, of all things visible and invisible.

    We believe in one Lord Jesus Christ, the only begotten Son of God, begotten of the Father before all ages, God from God, Light from Light, true God from true God, begotten, not created, of the same essence as the Father, Through whom all things were made.

    Who for us men and for our salvation came down from heaven and was incarnate by the Holy Spirit and the Virgin Mary, and became human. Who for us too was crucified under Pontius Pilate, suffered and was buried. The third day he rose again according to the Scriptures, ascended into heaven and is seated at the right hand of the Father. He will come again in glory to judge the living and the dead, and his kingdom will have no end.

We believe in the Holy Spirit, the Lord and life-giver, who proceeds from the Father and the Son, who together with the Father and the Son is worshipped and glorified, who spoke by the prophets.

We believe in one holy catholic and apostolic Church.

We acknowledge one baptism for the forgiveness of sin, and we look for the resurrection of the dead and the life of the age to come.

Amen.

7. The Lord's Prayer

Our Father in heaven,
Hallowed be your name;
Your kingdom come, Your will be done on earth as it is in heaven;
Give us this day our daily bread;
And forgive us our debts, as we also have forgiven our debtors;
And lead us not into temptation, but deliver us from evil;
For yours is the kingdom and the power and the glory forever.
Amen

THE DAILY READINGS

This daily reading schedule provides a three-year schedule for reading through the whole Bible.[6] This schedule provides a very reasonable pace for reading through the Bible. It has been marked according to regular calendar because the church year calendar varies on the number of weeks it includes, and so certain readings would be skipped-over depending on the year.

The schedule loosely follows the texts highlighted by the Revised Common Lectionary. The length of the readings varies to allow for the normal ebb and flow of busyness and activity that can vary over days, weeks, and months.

If you are looking an alternative to this plan, CTV highly recommends the *Chronological Reading Guide* produced by The Urban Ministry Institute. It is a one-year plan that follows the entire story of God as it occurred in historical order of events.[7]

A Prayer for the Reading of Scripture[8]

Most gracious God, our heavenly Father, in whom alone dwells all the fullness of light and wisdom, enlighten our minds by your Holy Spirit to truly understand your Word. Give us grace to receive it reverently and humbly. May it lead us to put our whole trust in you alone, and so to serve and honor you that we may glorify your holy name and encourage others by setting a good example.

John Calvin (Reformer and Theologian, 1509–1564)

---

[6] The Gospel of Mark, Romans, Ephesians, 1 and 2 Thessalonians, Titus, and Hebrews are each read twice in the three-year span.
[7] This plan is available through www.tumi.org.
[8] Taken from "Prayers for Reading the Bible" in *The Encyclopedia of Prayer and Praise*, Mark Water, Ed. (Hendrickson: 2004), 264.

December Daily Readings

Date	Year A	Year B	Year C
12/1	Matthew 1.1–17	Mark 1.1–28	Luke 1.1–25
12/2	Matthew 1.18–25	Mark 1.29–45	Luke 1.26–56
12/3	1 Peter 1	1 John 1	1 Thessalonians 1–2
12/4	Ezekiel 1	Jeremiah 1	Isaiah 1
12/5	Ezekiel 2	Jeremiah 2	Isaiah 2
12/6	Ezekiel 3	Jeremiah 3	Isaiah 3–4
12/7	Psalm 122	Psalm 2	Psalm 28
12/8	Matthew 2	Mark 2.1–12	Luke 1.57–80
12/9	Matthew 3	Mark 2.13–28	Luke 2.1–21
12/10	1 Peter 2	1 John 2	1 Thessalonians 3
12/11	Ezekiel 4	Jeremiah 4	Isaiah 5
12/12	Ezekiel 5	Jeremiah 5	Isaiah 6–7
12/13	Ezekiel 6	Jeremiah 6	Isaiah 8
12/14	Psalm 72	Psalm 103	*Luke 1.46–55 (Psalm)*
12/15	Matthew 4	Mark 3.1–19	Luke 2.22–40
12/16	Matthew 5.1–16	Mark 3.20–35	Luke 2.41–52
12/17	1 Peter 3	1 John 3	1 Thessalonians 4
12/18	Ezekiel 7	Jeremiah 7	Isaiah 9
12/19	Ezekiel 8	Jeremiah 8	Isaiah 10
12/20	Ezekiel 9	Jeremiah 9	Isaiah 11–12
12/21	Psalm 146	Psalm 126	Psalm 140
12/22	Matthew 5.17–48	Mark 4.1–20	Luke 3.1–22
12/23	Matthew 6	Mark 4.21–41	Luke 3.23–38
12/24	1 Peter 4	1 John 4	1 Thessalonians 5
12/25	Ezekiel 10	Jeremiah 10	Isaiah 13
12/26	Ezekiel 11	Jeremiah 11	Isaiah 14
12/27	Ezekiel 12	Jeremiah 12	Isaiah 15–16
12/28	Psalm 80	Luke 1.46–55	Psalm 76
12/29	Matthew 7.1–14	Mark 5.1–20	Luke 4.1–15
12/30	Matthew 7.15–29	Mark 5.21–43	Luke 4.16–44
12/31	1 Peter 5	1 John 5	Ephesians 1

January Daily Readings

Date	Year A	Year B	Year C
1/1	Ezekiel 13	Jeremiah 13	Isaiah 17–18
1/2	Ezekiel 14	Jeremiah 14	Isaiah 19
1/3	Ezekiel 15	Jeremiah 15	Isaiah 20–21
1/4	Psalm 147	Psalm 18	Psalm 64
1/5	Matthew 8.1–17	Mark 6.1–29	Luke 5.1–26
1/6	Matthew 8.18–34	Mark 6.30–56	Luke 5.27–39
1/7	2 Peter 1	2, 3 John	Ephesians 2
1/8	Ezekiel 16	Jeremiah 16	Isaiah 22
1/9	Ezekiel 17	Jeremiah 17	Isaiah 23
1/10	Ezekiel 18	Jeremiah 18	Isaiah 24
1/11	Psalm 84	Psalm 58	Psalm 143
1/12	Matthew 9.1–17	Mark 7.1–23	Luke 6.1–19
1/13	Matthew 9.18–38	Mark 7.24–37	Luke 6.20–49
1/14	2 Peter 2	Titus 1	Ephesians 3
1/15	Ezekiel 19	Jeremiah 19	Isaiah 25–26
1/16	Ezekiel 20	Jeremiah 20	Isaiah 27
1/17	Ezekiel 21	Jeremiah 21	Isaiah 28
1/18	Psalm 29	Psalm 73	Psalm 36
1/19	Matthew 10.1–25	Mark 8.1–26	Luke 7.1–17
1/20	Matthew 10.26–42	Mark 8.27 — 9.1	Luke 7.18–50
1/21	2 Peter 3	Titus 2	Ephesians 4
1/22	Ezekiel 22	Jeremiah 22	Isaiah 29
1/23	Ezekiel 23	Jeremiah 23	Isaiah 30
1/24	Ezekiel 24	Jeremiah 24	Isaiah 31–32
1/25	Psalm 40	Psalm 62	Psalm 38
1/26	Matthew 11.1–19	Mark 9.2–29	Luke 8.1–21
1/27	Matthew 11.20–30	Mark 9.30–50	Luke 8.22–56
1/28	Jude	Titus 3	Ephesians 5
1/29	Ezekiel 25	Jeremiah 25	Isaiah 33
1/30	Ezekiel 26	Jeremiah 26	Isaiah 34–35
1/31	Ezekiel 27	Jeremiah 27	Isaiah 36

February Daily Readings

Date	Year A	Year B	Year C
2/1	Psalm 27	Psalm 111	Psalm 71
2/2	Matthew 12.1–21	Mark 10.1–31	Luke 9.1–17
2/3	Matthew 12.22–50	Mark 10.32–52	Luke 9.18–45
2/4	Hebrews 1	Romans 1	Ephesians 6
2/5	Ezekiel 28	Jeremiah 28	Isaiah 37
2/6	Ezekiel 29	Jeremiah 29	Isaiah 38–39
2/7	Ezekiel 30	Jeremiah 30	Isaiah 40
2/8	Psalm 15	Psalm 3	Psalm 141
2/9	Matthew 13.1–23	Mark 11.1–11	Luke 9.46–62
2/10	Matthew 13.24–58	Mark 11.12–33	Luke 10.1–24
2/11	Hebrews 2	Romans 2	1 Corinthians 1
2/12	Ezekiel 31	Jeremiah 31	Isaiah 41
2/13	Ezekiel 32	Jeremiah 32	Isaiah 42
2/14	Ezekiel 33	Jeremiah 33	Isaiah 43
2/15	Psalm 112	Psalm 30	Psalm 93
2/16	Matthew 14.1–21	Mark 12.1–17	Luke 10.25–42
2/17	Matthew 14.22–36	Mark 12.18–44	Luke 11.1–36
2/18	Hebrews 3	Romans 3	1 Corinthians 2
2/19	Ezekiel 34	Jeremiah 34	Isaiah 44
2/20	Ezekiel 35	Jeremiah 35	Isaiah 45
2/21	Ezekiel 36	Jeremiah 36	Isaiah 46–47
2/22	Psalm 131	Psalm 41	Psalm 37
2/23	Matthew 15.1–20	Mark 13.1–23	Luke 11.37–54
2/24	Matthew 15.21–39	Mark 13.24–37	Luke 12.1–34
2/25	Hebrews 4	Romans 4	1 Corinthians 3
2/26	Ezekiel 37	Jeremiah 37	Isaiah 48
2/27	Ezekiel 38	Jeremiah 38	Isaiah 49
2/28	Ezekiel 39	Jeremiah 39	Isaiah 50–51

March Daily Readings

Date	Year A	Year B	Year C
3/1	Psalm 32	Psalm 50	Psalm 74
3/2	Matthew 16	Mark 14.1–31	Luke 12.35–59
3/3	Matthew 17	Mark 14.32–72	Luke 13.1–17
3/4	Hebrews 5	Romans 5	1 Corinthians 4
3/5	Ezekiel 40	Jeremiah 40	Isaiah 52–53
3/6	Ezekiel 41	Jeremiah 41	Isaiah 54
3/7	Ezekiel 42	Jeremiah 42	Isaiah 55–56
3/8	Psalm 121	Psalm 25	Psalm 94
3/9	Matthew 18.1–20	Mark 15	Luke 13.18–35
3/10	Matthew 18.21–35	Mark 16	Luke 14.1–24
3/11	Hebrews 6	Romans 6	1 Corinthians 5–6
3/12	Ezekiel 43	Jeremiah 43	Isaiah 57
3/13	Ezekiel 44	Jeremiah 44	Isaiah 58
3/14	Ezekiel 45	Jeremiah 45	Isaiah 59
3/15	Psalm 95	Psalm 22	Psalm 128
3/16	Matthew 19.1–15	Mark 1	Luke 14.25–35
3/17	Matthew 19.16–30	Mark 2	Luke 15
3/18	Hebrews 7	Romans 7	1 Corinthians 7
3/19	Ezekiel 46	Jeremiah 46	Isaiah 60
3/20	Ezekiel 47	Jeremiah 47	Isaiah 61–62
3/21	Ezekiel 48	Jeremiah 48	Isaiah 63–64
3/22	Psalm 130	Psalm 6	Psalm 63
3/23	Matthew 20.1–16	Mark 3	Luke 16.1–13
3/24	Matthew 20.17–34	Mark 4	Luke 16.14–31
3/25	Hebrews 8	Romans 8	1 Corinthians 8
3/26	Daniel 1	Jeremiah 49	Isaiah 65
3/27	Daniel 2	Jeremiah 50	Isaiah 66
3/28	Daniel 3	Jeremiah 51	Amos 1
3/29	Psalm 31	Psalms 9–10	Psalm 69
3/30	Matthew 21.1–17	Mark 5.1–20	Luke 17.1–19
3/31	Matthew 21.18–46	Mark 5.21–43	Luke 17.20–37

April Daily Readings

Date	Year A	Year B	Year C
4/1	Hebrews 9	Romans 9	1 Corinthians 9
4/2	Daniel 4	Jeremiah 52	Amos 2
4/3	Daniel 5	Lamentations 1	Amos 3–4
4/4	Daniel 6	Lamentations 2	Amos 5
4/5	Psalm 118	Psalm 51	Psalm 101
4/6	Matthew 22.1–22	Mark 6	Luke 18.1–17
4/7	Matthew 22.23–46	Mark 7	Luke 18.18–43
4/8	Hebrews 10.1–18	Romans 10	1 Corinthians 10
4/9	Daniel 7	Lamentations 3	Amos 6–7
4/10	Daniel 8	Lamentations 4	Amos 8–9
4/11	Daniel 9	Lamentations 5	Hosea 1
4/12	Psalm 16	Psalm 56	Psalm 39
4/13	Matthew 23.1–22	Mark 8.1–9.1	Luke 19.1–27
4/14	Matthew 23.23–39	Mark 9.2–50	Luke 19.28–48
4/15	Hebrews 10.19–40	Romans 11	1 Corinthians 11
4/16	Daniel 10	Jonah 1	Hosea 2
4/17	Daniel 11	Jonah 2	Hosea 3–4
4/18	Daniel 12	Jonah 3	Hosea 5–6
4/19	Psalm 116	Psalm 61	Psalm 86
4/20	Matthew 24.1–31	Mark 10.1–31	Luke 20.1–18
4/21	Matthew 24.32–51	Mark 10.32–52	Luke 20.19–47
4/22	Hebrews 11.1–22	Romans 12	1 Corinthians 12
4/23	Zechariah 1	Jonah 4	Hosea 7–8
4/24	Zechariah 2	Micah 1	Hosea 9
4/25	Zechariah 3–4	Micah 2	Hosea 10–11
4/26	Psalm 23	Psalm 4	Psalm 134
4/27	Matthew 25.1–30	Mark 11	Luke 21.1–19
4/28	Matthew 25.31–46	Mark 12	Luke 21.20–38
4/29	Hebrews 11.23–39	Romans 13	1 Corinthians 13
4/30	Zechariah 5	Micah 3	Hosea 12

May Daily Readings

Date	Year A	Year B	Year C
5/1	Zechariah 6	Micah 4	Hosea 13
5/2	Zechariah 7	Micah 5	Hosea 14
5/3	Psalm 66	Psalm 21	Psalm 148
5/4	Matthew 26.1–46	Mark 13.1–23	Luke 22.1–46
5/5	Matthew 26.47–75	Mark 13.24–37	Luke 22.47–71
5/6	Hebrews 12.1–11	Romans 14	1 Corinthians 14
5/7	Zechariah 8	Micah 6	Nahum 1
5/8	Zechariah 9	Micah 7	Nahum 2
5/9	Zechariah 10	Obadiah	Nahum 3
5/10	Psalm 68	Psalm 98	Psalm 67
5/11	Matthew 27.1–26	Mark 14.1–42	Luke 23.1–25
5/12	Matthew 27.27–56	Mark 14.43–72	Luke 23.26–56
5/13	Hebrews 12.12–29	Romans 15	1 Corinthians 15
5/14	Zechariah 11	Haggai 1	Habakkuk 1
5/15	Zechariah 12–13	Haggai 2	Habakkuk 2
5/16	Zechariah 14	Haggai 3	Habakkuk 3
5/17	Psalm 104	Psalm 1	Psalm 92
5/18	Matthew 27.58–66	Mark 15	Luke 24.1–35
5/19	Matthew 28	Mark 16	Luke 24.36–53
5/20	Hebrews 13	Romans 16	1 Corinthians 16
5/21	Joel 1	Malachi 1	Zephaniah 1
5/22	Joel 2	Malachi 2	Zephaniah 2
5/23	Joel 3	Malachi 3–4	Zephaniah 3
5/24	Psalm 8	Psalm 33	Psalm 60
5/25	John 1	Revelation 1	Acts 1–2
5/26	Romans 1	2 Corinthians 1	Galatians 1
5/27	Genesis 1	Joshua 1–2	1 Chronicles 1–2
5/28	Genesis 2	Joshua 3–4	1 Chronicles 3–4
5/29	Genesis 3	Joshua 5–6	1 Chronicles 5–6
5/30	Genesis 4–5	Joshua 7	1 Chronicles 7–8
5/31	Psalm 119.1–40	Psalm 81	Psalm 96

June Daily Readings

Date	Year A	Year B	Year C
6/1	John 2	Revelation 2.1–11	Acts 3
6/2	Romans 2	2 Corinthians 2–3	Galatians 2
6/3	Genesis 6–7	Joshua 8	1 Chronicles 9
6/4	Genesis 8–9	Joshua 9	1 Chronicles 10–11
6/5	Genesis 10–11	Joshua 10	1 Chronicles 12
6/6	Genesis 12–13	Joshua 11–12	1 Chronicles 13–14
6/7	Ps. 119.41–80	Psalm 138	Psalm 108
6/8	John 3	Revelation 2.12–29	Acts 4
6/9	Romans 3	2 Corinthians 4–5	Galatians 3
6/10	Genesis 14–15	Joshua 13	1 Chronicles 15–16
6/11	Genesis 16–17	Joshua 14–15	1 Chronicles 17–18
6/12	Genesis 18–19	Joshua 16–17	1 Chronicles 19–20
6/13	Genesis 20–21	Joshua 18–19	1 Chronicles 21–22
6/14	Ps. 119.81–120	Psalm 20	Psalm 5
6/15	John 4.1–26	Revelation 3	Acts 5
6/16	Romans 4	2 Corinthians 6–7	Galatians 4
6/17	Genesis 22–23	Joshua 20–21	1 Chronicles 23–24
6/18	Genesis 24	Joshua 22	1 Chronicles 25–26
6/19	Genesis 25–26	Joshua 23–24	1 Chronicles 27–28
6/20	Genesis 27	Judges 1	1 Chronicles 29
6/21	Ps. 119.121–152	Psalm 91	Psalms 42–43
6/22	John 4.27–54	Revelation 4	Acts 6
6/23	Romans 5	2 Corinthians 8–9	Galatians 5
6/24	Genesis 28–29	Judges 2	2 Chronicles 1–2
6/25	Genesis 30	Judges 3	2 Chronicles 3–4
6/26	Genesis 31–32	Judges 4–5	2 Chronicles 5–6
6/27	Genesis 33–34	Judges 6	2 Chronicles 7–8
6/28	Ps. 119.153–176	Psalm 102	Psalm 77
6/29	John 5	Revelation 5	Acts 7
6/30	Romans 6	2 Corinthians 10	Galatians 6

July Daily Readings

Date	Year A	Year B	Year C
7/1	Genesis 35–36	Judges 7–8	2 Chronicles 9–10
7/2	Genesis 37–38	Judges 9	2 Chronicles 11–12
7/3	Genesis 39–40	Judges 10	2 Chronicles 13–14
7/4	Genesis 41	Judges 11–12	2 Chronicles 15–16
7/5	Psalm 13	Psalm 48	Psalm 2
7/6	John 6.1–24	Revelation 6	Acts 8
7/7	Romans 7	2 Corinthians 11	Colossians 1
7/8	Genesis 42	Judges 13	2 Chronicles 17–18
7/9	Genesis 43–44	Judges 14–15	2 Chronicles 19–20
7/10	Genesis 45–46	Judges 16–17	2 Chronicles 21–22
7/11	Genesis 47–48	Judges 18–19	2 Chronicles 23–24
7/12	Psalm 45	Psalm 24	Psalm 82
7/13	John 6.25–71	Revelation 7	Acts 9
7/14	Romans 8	2 Corinthians 12–13	Colossians 2
7/15	Genesis 49–50	Judges 20	2 Chronicles 25–26
7/16	Exodus 1–2	Judges 21	2 Chronicles 27–28
7/17	Exodus 3–4	Ruth 1–2	2 Chronicles 29
7/18	Exodus 5–6	Ruth 3–4	2 Chronicles 30–31
7/19	Psalm 139	Psalm 89	Psalm 52
7/20	John 7.1–24	Revelation 8	Acts 10
7/21	Romans 9	Ephesians 1	Colossians 3
7/22	Exodus 7–8	1 Samuel 1	2 Chronicles 32
7/23	Exodus 9–10	1 Samuel 2	2 Chronicles 33–34
7/24	Exodus 11–12	1 Samuel 3	2 Chronicles 35–36
7/25	Exodus 13–14	1 Samuel 4–5	Ezra 1–2
7/26	Psalm 105	Psalm 14	Psalm 142
7/27	John 7.25–52	Revelation 9	Acts 11
7/28	Romans 10	Ephesians 2	Colossians 4
7/29	Exodus 15	1 Samuel 6–7	Ezra 3–4
7/30	Exodus 16–17	1 Samuel 8–9	Ezra 5–6
7/31	Exodus 18–19	1 Samuel 10	Ezra 7

August Daily Readings

Date	Year A	Year B	Year C
8/1	Exodus 20	1 Samuel 11–12	Ezra 8
8/2	Psalm 17	Psalm 110	Psalm 49
8/3	John 8.1–30	Revelation 10	Acts 12
8/4	Romans 11	Ephesians 3	Philemon
8/5	Exodus 21–22	1 Samuel 13	Ezra 9–10
8/6	Exodus 23–24	1 Samuel 14	Nehemiah 1–2
8/7	Exodus 25–26	1 Samuel 15–16	Nehemiah 3
8/8	Exodus 27–28	1 Samuel 17	Nehemiah 4–5
8/9	Psalm 85	Psalm 34	Psalm 55
8/10	John 8.31–59	Revelation 11	Acts 13
8/11	Romans 12	Ephesians 4	1 Timothy 1
8/12	Exodus 29	1 Samuel 18–19	Nehemiah 6
8/13	Exodus 30–31	1 Samuel 20	Nehemiah 7
8/14	Exodus 32–33	1 Samuel 21–22	Nehemiah 8
8/15	Exodus 34	1 Samuel 23–24	Nehemiah 9
8/16	Psalm 133	Psalm 53	Psalm 12
8/17	John 9	Revelation 12	Acts 14
8/18	Romans 13	Ephesians 5	1 Timothy 2
8/19	Exodus 35–36	1 Samuel 25	Nehemiah 10
8/20	Exodus 37–38	1 Samuel 26–27	Nehemiah 11
8/21	Exodus 39–40	1 Samuel 28–29	Nehemiah 12
8/22	Leviticus 1–2	1 Samuel 30–31	Nehemiah 13
8/23	Psalm 124	Psalm 109	Psalm 87
8/24	John 10	Revelation 13.1–10	Acts 15
8/25	Romans 14	Ephesians 6	1 Timothy 3
8/26	Leviticus 1–2	2 Samuel 1–2	Esther 1
8/27	Leviticus 3–4	2 Samuel 3–4	Esther 2
8/28	Leviticus 5–6	2 Samuel 5–6	Esther 3–4
8/29	Leviticus 7	2 Samuel 7–8	Esther 5–6
8/30	Psalm 26	Psalm 35	Psalm 120

September Daily Readings

Date	Year A	Year B	Year C
9/1	John 11	Revelation 13.11–18	Acts 16
9/2	Romans 15	James 1–2	1 Timothy 4
9/3	Leviticus 8–9	2 Samuel 9–10	Esther 7–8
9/4	Leviticus 10–11	2 Samuel 11–12	Esther 9–10
9/5	Leviticus 12–13	2 Samuel 13–14	Job 1–2
9/6	Leviticus 14	2 Samuel 15–16	Job 3
9/7	Psalm 149	Psalm 125	Psalm 113
9/8	John 12.1–19	Revelation 14.1–12	Acts 17
9/9	Romans 16	James 3–4	1 Timothy 5
9/10	Leviticus 15–16	2 Samuel 17–18	Job 4–5
9/11	Leviticus 17–18	2 Samuel 19	Job 6–7
9/12	Leviticus 19–20	2 Samuel 20–21	Job 8–9
9/13	Leviticus 21–22	2 Samuel 22	Job 10–11
9/14	Psalm 114	Psalm 11	Psalm 79
9/15	John 12.20–50	Revelation 14.13–20	Acts 18
9/16	Philippians 1	James 5	1 Timothy 6
9/17	Leviticus 23	2 Samuel 23–24	Job 12
9/18	Leviticus 24–25	1 Kings 1	Job 13–14
9/19	Leviticus 26–27	1 Kings 2–3	Job 15
9/20	Numbers 1	1 Kings 4–5	Job 16–17
9/21	Psalm 145	Psalm 54	Psalm 57
9/22	John 13	Revelation 15	Acts 19
9/23	Philippians 2	Hebrews 1	2 Timothy 1
9/24	Numbers 2–3	1 Kings 6	Job 18–19
9/25	Numbers 4	1 Kings 7	Job 20
9/26	Numbers 5–6	1 Kings 8	Job 21–22
9/27	Numbers 7	1 Kings 9–10	Job 23–24
9/28	Psalm 78	Psalm 7	Psalm 137
9/29	John 14	Revelation 16	Acts 20
9/30	Philippians 3	Hebrews 2	2 Timothy 2

October Daily Readings

Date	Year A	Year B	Year C
10/1	Numbers 8–9	1 Kings 11	Job 25–26
10/2	Numbers 10–11	1 Kings 12–13	Job 27–28
10/3	Numbers 12–13	1 Kings 14–15	Job 29–30
10/4	Numbers 14	1 Kings 16–17	Job 31
10/5	Psalm 19	Psalm 144	Psalm 117
10/6	John 15	Revelation 17	Acts 21
10/7	Philippians 4	Hebrews 3	2 Timothy 3
10/8	Numbers 15	1 Kings 18–19	Job 32–33
10/9	Numbers 16	1 Kings 20	Job 34
10/10	Numbers 17–18	1 Kings 21	Job 35–36
10/11	Numbers 19–20	1 Kings 22	Job 37
10/12	Psalm 106	Psalm 129	Psalm 88
10/13	John 16	Revelation 18	Acts 22
10/14	1 Thessalonians 1–2	Hebrews 4	2 Timothy 4
10/15	Numbers 21–22	2 Kings 1–2	Job 38
10/16	Numbers 23–24	2 Kings 3–4	Job 39–40
10/17	Numbers 25–26	2 Kings 5	Job 41–42
10/18	Numbers 27–28	2 Kings 6	Proverbs 1–2
10/19	Psalm 99	Psalm 97	Psalm 65
10/20	John 17	Revelation 19.1–10	Acts 23
10/21	1 Thessalonians 3	Hebrews 5–6	Titus 1
10/22	Numbers 29–30	2 Kings 7–8	Proverbs 3
10/23	Numbers 31	2 Kings 9	Proverbs 4–5
10/24	Numbers 32	2 Kings 10	Proverbs 6–7
10/25	Numbers 33–34	2 Kings 11–12	Proverbs 8–9
10/26	Psalm 90	Psalm 115	Psalm 75
10/27	John 18	Revelation 19.11–21	Acts 24
10/28	1 Thessalonians 4	Hebrews 7	Titus 2
10/29	Numbers 35–36	2 Kings 13–14	Proverbs 10
10/30	Deuteronomy 1	2 Kings 15	Proverbs 11
10/31	Deuteronomy 2–3	2 Kings 16	Proverbs 12

November Daily Readings

Date	Year A	Year B	Year C
11/1	Deuteronomy 4	2 Kings 17	Proverbs 13
11/2	Psalm 107	Psalm 135	Psalm 59
11/3	John 19.1–16	Revelation 20	Acts 25
11/4	1 Thessalonians 5	Hebrews 8–9	Titus 3
11/5	Deuteronomy 5–6	2 Kings 18	Proverbs 14
11/6	Deuteronomy 7–8	2 Kings 19	Proverbs 15
11/7	Deuteronomy 9–10	2 Kings 20	Proverbs 16
11/8	Deuteronomy 11–12	2 Kings 21–22	Proverbs 17
11/9	Psalm 70	Psalm 83	Psalm 44
11/10	John 19.17–42	Revelation 21.1–21	Acts 26
11/11	2 Thessalonians 1	Hebrews 10	2 Thessalonians 1
11/12	Deuteronomy 13–14	2 Kings 23	Proverbs 18–19
11/13	Deuteronomy 15	2 Kings 24–25	Proverbs 20
11/14	Deuteronomy 16–17	Ecclesiastes 1–2	Proverbs 21
11/15	Deuteronomy 18–19	Ecclesiastes 3–4	Proverbs 22
11/16	Psalm 123	Psalm 127	Psalm 136
11/17	John 20	Revelation 21.22–22.7	Acts 27
11/18	2 Thessalonians 2	Hebrews 11	2 Thessalonians 2
11/19	Deuteronomy 20–21	Ecclesiastes 5–6	Proverbs 23
11/20	Deuteronomy 22–23	Ecclesiastes 7–8	Proverbs 24
11/21	Deuteronomy 24–25	Ecclesiastes 9–10	Proverbs 25–26
11/22	Deuteronomy 26–27	Ecclesiastes 11–12	Proverbs 27
11/23	Psalm 100	Psalm 47	Psalm 1
11/24	John 21	Revelation 22.8–21	Acts 28
11/25	2 Thessalonians 3	Hebrews 12–13	2 Thessalonians 3
11/26	Deuteronomy 28	Song of Songs 1–2	Proverbs 28
11/27	Deuteronomy 29–30	Song of Songs 3–4	Proverbs 29
11/28	Deuteronomy 31–32	Song of Songs 5–6	Proverbs 30
11/29	Deuteronomy 33–34	Song of Songs 7–8	Proverbs 31
11/30	Psalm 150	Psalm 132	Psalm 46

PRAYERS

The Lord's Prayer (Matthew 6.9–13, ESV)

Our Father in heaven,
Hallowed be your name;
Your kingdom come, your will be done on earth as it is in heaven;
Give us this day our daily bread;
And forgive us our debts, as we also have forgiven our debtors;
And lead us not into temptation, but deliver us from evil;
For yours is the kingdom and the power and the glory forever.
Amen[9]

Explanation of the Parts of the Lord's Prayer

❖ *Our Father in heaven* – Recognition of the Lord: We recognize the gracious character and exalted position of the One we address.

❖ *Hallowed be your name* – God's Glory: We acknowledge the Lord as holy (hallowed), ask Him to make his glory (his name) known and recognized on the earth.

❖ *Your kingdom come, your will be done on earth as it is in heaven* – Desire for God's Purposes: We ask God to fulfill his purposes and plans on the earth, and we submit to his will for us. We declare our trust in God's goodness and control, and bring requests for the expansion of his kingdom rule.

❖ *Give us this day our daily bread* – Dependence on God's Provision: We recognize that all of us depend on the Lord for everything, even the most basic needs, and bring

---

[9] In the ESV, the phrase "For yours is the kingdom and the power and the glory, forever. Amen" appears in the footnote of Matthew 6.13.

requests of provision to God on behalf of others and ourselves.

❖ *And forgive us our debts, as we also have forgiven our debtors* – Our Repentance and Kingdom Relationships: We recognize that we are sinners who depend on the grace and mercy of the Lord. We confess our sins, and ask for help in extending God's grace and mercy to others.

❖ *And lead us not into temptation, but deliver us from evil* – Our Purity and Protection: We ask the Lord to protect us from Satan's attempts to derail us in sin, and to harm us physically and spiritually.

❖ *For yours is the kingdom and the power and the glory forever, Amen* – Our Submission: We submit ourselves to the fact that the earth is the Lord's, and everything in it, all glory and honor are due him; we claim none for ourselves but give it all to him.

The Jesus Prayer

Lord Jesus Christ, Son of God, have mercy on me, a sinner.

Based on Luke 18.13

The Story of God[10]

Eternal God our Lord you are the creator and ruler of all things. In pride, Satan rebelled against you and ignited a cosmic war. Though we were created in your own image, we joined the rebellion by obeying Satan, the ancient serpent. In our sin we were separated from you and fell under the power of the evil one. Your creation was plunged into darkness and subjected to death. Lord, in your infinite mercy, you promised to send a Savior to crush evil and redeem a people for yourself. In the fullness of time, you sent your own Son,

---

[10] Taken from the CTV *Liturgy of the Sacred Service* (pp.146–47)

Jesus, down from heaven to invade the dark realm of Satan. Through Christ's life, death, resurrection, and ascension, you defeated the devil and opened the kingdom of heaven to all believers. Very soon, you will send your Son again to this world and he will completely conquer Satan and all demonic activity. He will destroy sin and death and establish your eternal kingdom.

You are God (Te Deum)

You are God: we praise you; You are the Lord: we acclaim you;
You are the eternal Father: all creation worships you.
To you all angels, all the powers of heaven,
Cherubim and Seraphim, sing in endless praise:
Holy, holy, holy Lord, God of power and might,
heaven and earth are full of your glory.
The glorious company of apostles praise you.
The noble fellowship of prophets praise you.
The white robed army of martyrs praise you.
Throughout the world the holy Church acclaims you;
Father, of majesty unbounded,
your true and only Son, worthy of all worship,
and the Holy Spirit, advocate and guide.
You, Christ, are the King of glory, the eternal Son of the Father.
When you became human to set us free
you did not shun the Virgin's womb.
You overcame the sting of death
and opened the kingdom of heaven to all believers.
You are seated at God's right hand in glory.
We believe that you will come and be our judge.
Come then, Lord, and help your people,
bought with the price of your own blood,
and bring us with your saints to glory everlasting.

Situational Prayers[11]

A Prayer of Self Dedication

Almighty and eternal God, draw our hearts to you, guide our minds, fill our imaginations, and control our wills, so that we may be completely yours, utterly dedicated to you; and then use us, we pray, as you desire, always for your glory and for the welfare of your church; through our Lord and Savior Jesus Christ. Amen.

A Prayer of St. Francis for Representing Christ in the World

Lord, make us instruments of your peace. Where there is hatred, let us sow love; where there is injury, pardon; where there is discord, union; where there is doubt, faith; where there is despair, hope; where there is darkness, light; where there is sadness, joy. Grant that we may not so much seek to be consoled as to console; to be understood as to understand; to be loved as to love. For it is in giving that we receive; it is in pardoning that we are pardoned; and it is in dying that we are born to eternal life. Amen.

Confession of Sin[12]

Most merciful God, we confess that we have sinned against you in thought, word, and deed, by what we have done, and by what we have left undone. We have not loved you with our whole heart; we have not loved our neighbors as ourselves. We are truly sorry and we humbly repent, for the sake of your Son Jesus Christ, have mercy on us and forgive us; that we may delight in your will, and walk in your ways, to the glory of your Name.

---

[11] Unless otherwise noted, these prayers are adapted from the Prayers and Thanksgivings of *The Book of Common Prayer*, 1979 Ed.
[12] Taken from the CTV *Liturgy of the Sacred Service* (p.145).

When Facing Temptation[13]

Strengthen my life, Lord, against every temptation, and turn my adversary [the Devil] away from me ashamed and confounded every time he attacks me. Strengthen every step of my mind and tongue, and every move of my body.

John Chrysostom (Pastor and Theologian, c.347–407)

The Assurance of Forgiveness and Peace with God[14]

Gracious Father, you sent your Son to destroy the works of the devil. You made us alive together with him, having forgiven our sin, by canceling the record of debt that stood against us, nailing it to the cross. You disarmed the rulers and authorities and put them to open shame, by triumphing over them in Christ's death and resurrection. We now draw near to your throne with confidence, knowing that we will receive mercy and find grace. Amen.

For the Church

Gracious Father, we pray for your holy apostolic Church. Fill it with all your truth, all the love of Christ, and all the power of your Spirit. Where it is corrupt, purify it; where it is in error, direct it; where in anything it is amiss, reform it. Where it is right, strengthen it; where it is in want, provide for it; where it is divided, reunite it; may your kingdom come, may your victory be known for the sake of Jesus Christ your Son, our Savior. Amen.

For the Mission of the Church

Ever-living God, it is your will that all should come to you through your Son Jesus Christ. Inspire our witness to him, that all may know the power of his forgiveness, the hope of his resurrection, and may experience his victory over sin, death, and Satan; through Christ our

---

[13] Taken from "Resisting Temptation" *The Encyclopedia of Prayer and Praise*, 139.
[14] From the CTV *Liturgy of the Sacred Service* (p. 146)

Lord who lives and reigns with you and the Holy Spirit, one God, now and forever. Amen.

For the Unity of the Church

O God the Father of our Lord Jesus Christ, our only Savior, the Prince of Peace: Give us grace to see clearly the danger of being divided; take away all hatred and prejudice, and whatever else may hinder us from godly unity; so that, as there is but one Body and one Spirit, one hope of our calling, one Lord, one Faith, one Baptism, one God and Father of us all, so we may be all of one heart and of one soul, united in one holy bond of truth and peace, of faith and charity, and may with one mind and one voice glorify you; through Jesus Christ our Lord. Amen.

A Prayer for the Reading of Scripture[15]

Most gracious God, our heavenly Father, in whom alone dwells all the fullness of light and wisdom, enlighten our minds by your Holy Spirit to truly understand your Word. Give us grace to receive it reverently and humbly. May it lead us to put our whole trust in you alone, and so to serve and honor you that we may glorify your holy name and encourage others by setting a good example.

John Calvin (Reformer and Theologian, 1509–1564)

For Peace

Eternal God, in whose perfect kingdom no weapon is drawn but the sword of righteousness, no strength known but the strength of love: So mightily spread abroad your Spirit, that all peoples may be gathered under the banner of the Prince of Peace, as children of one Father; to whom be dominion and glory, now and forever. Amen.

---

[15] Taken from "Prayers for Reading the Bible" in *The Encyclopedia of Prayer and Praise,* Mark Water, Ed. (Hendrickson: 2004), 264.

For Our Country

Almighty God, who has given us this good country: We humbly ask you that we may always prove ourselves a people mindful of your favor and glad to do your will. Bless our land with honorable business, sound leadership, and pure laws. Save us from violence, hatred, and confusion; from pride and arrogance, and from every evil way. Defend our freedom, and fashion into one united people the multitudes brought here out of many nations and tongues. Give the spirit of wisdom to those whom, in your Name, we entrust the authority of government, that there may be justice and peace at home, and that, through obedience to your law, we may show forth your praise among the nations of the earth. In the time of prosperity, fill our hearts with thankfulness, and in the day of trouble, do not allow our trust in you to fail; all of this we ask through Jesus Christ our Lord. Amen.

For Social Justice

Grant, O God, that your holy and life-giving Spirit may so move every human heart (and especially the hearts of the people of this land), that barriers which divide us may crumble, suspicions disappear, and hatred cease; that our divisions being healed, we may live in the justice and peace that mark your kingdom; through Jesus Christ our Lord. Amen.

For Cities

Heavenly Father, in your Word you have given us a vision of that holy City to which the nations of the world bring their glory: Behold and visit, we pray, the cities of the earth. Renew the ties of mutual care which form our societies. Send us honest and able leaders. Enable us to address poverty, prejudice, and oppression, that peace may prevail with righteousness, and justice with order, and that men and women from different cultures and with differing talents may regard one another with respect as fellow human beings; through Jesus Christ our Lord. Amen.

For the Unemployed

Heavenly Father, we lift up before you those who suffer want and anxiety from lack of work. Guide the people of this land so to use our public and private wealth that all may find suitable and fulfilling employment, and receive just payment for their labor; through Jesus Christ our Lord. Amen.

For the Poor and the Neglected

Almighty and most merciful God, we lift up before you all poor and neglected persons whom it would be easy for us to forget: the homeless and the destitute, the old and the sick, and all who have none to care for them. Help us to heal those who are broken in body or spirit, to turn their sorrow into joy, to help them experience the victory that your Son has won through his death and resurrection. Grant this, Father, for the love of your Son, who for our sake became poor, Jesus Christ our Lord. Amen.

For Those in Prison

Lord Jesus, for our sake you were condemned as a criminal: Visit our jails and prisons with your compassion and judgment. Remember all prisoners, and bring the guilty to repentance and new life according to your will, and give them hope for their future. When any are held unjustly, bring them release; forgive us, and teach us to improve our justice. Remember those who work in these institutions; keep them humane and compassionate; and save them from becoming brutal or callous. And since what we do for those in prison, O Lord, we do for you, help us to care for them. All this we ask for your mercy's sake. Amen.

For Families

Almighty God, our heavenly Father, who places the lonely in families: We commend to your continual care the homes in which your people dwell. Put far from them, we ask you, every root of bitterness, every thought of infidelity, the idolatry of greed, and the pride of life. Fill them with faith, virtue, knowledge, temperance, patience, godliness. Knit together in constant affection those who, in holy marriage, have been made one flesh. Turn the hearts of the parents to the children, and the hearts of the children to the parents; and so enkindle fervent love among us all, that we may forever be kindhearted one to another; through Jesus Christ our Lord. Amen.

For Parents (or Any Who Care for Children)

Almighty God, heavenly Father, you have blessed us with the joy and care of children: Give us calm strength and patient wisdom as we bring them up, that we may teach them to love whatever is just and true and good, following the example of our Savior Jesus Christ. Amen.

For Travelers

O God, our heavenly Father, whose glory fills the whole creation, and whose presence we find wherever we go: Preserve those who travel (in particular _____); surround them with your loving care; protect them from every danger; and bring them in safety to their journey's end; through Jesus Christ our Lord. Amen.

For the Sick

O Father of mercies and God of all comfort, our only help in time of need: We humbly ask you to look upon, visit, and relieve your sick servant _____ for whom we now pray. Look upon (him/her) with the eyes of your mercy; comfort (him/her) with a sense of your goodness; preserve (him/her) from the temptations of the enemy; and give (him/her) patience under (his/her) affliction. In your good time, restore (him/her) to health, and enable (him/her) to lead the rest of (his/her) life in holy fear, to your glory; and grant that finally (he/she) may dwell with you in life everlasting; through Jesus Christ our Lord. Amen.

For the Victims of Addiction

O blessed Lord, you ministered to all who came to you: Look with compassion upon all who through addiction have lost their health and freedom. Restore to them the assurance of your unfailing mercy; remove from them the fears that haunt them; strengthen them in the work of their recovery and allow them to know your victory; and to those who care for them, give patient understanding and persevering love. Amen.

For Those in Trouble or Bereavement

O merciful Father, you have taught us in your holy Word that you do not willingly afflict or grieve human beings. Look with pity upon the sorrows of your servants for whom our prayers are offered. Remember them, O Lord, in mercy, nourish their souls with patience, comfort them with a sense of your goodness, lift up your countenance upon them, and give them peace; through Jesus Christ our Lord. Amen.

4

THE CHURCH YEAR

INTRODUCTION

"The Church Year is an ancient means by which the Church through the ages has identified itself with the Story of God in Christ."[16] Through the church year, Christians walk with Christ through his coming, his life, suffering, death, and resurrection, to his ascension and sending of the Holy Spirit. Each season helps us experience a different aspect of Christ's person and work. Through identifying with Jesus in all phases of his incarnation, we are enabled to participate with Christ in his life, and live out our union with Him in a new way.

The *Church Year At-A-Glance* is a helpful road map for the church year that will guide you as you journey together through the life of our Lord, and includes a theme verse for each season. We have also provided the specific dates and information necessary to navigate the church year for 2014–2034.[17]

The *Church Year Weekly Guide* provides the necessary information for a church to follow the church year. Each season of the church year is given at the top of the page with its general theme. For each week, the seasonal color and the Sunday texts of the Revised Common Lectionary (RCL) are given.

On many Sundays, the RCL gives options and portions of texts that may be read. We have chosen a particular course through the RCL for this book. During the first half of the year, the Cycles of Light and Life (Advent–Pentecost), we have followed the thematic lectionary which coordinates the Old Testament, Psalm, and New Testament readings with the theme of the Gospel text. So then, the lectionary topics connect all four passages. During Kingdomtide, we have followed the continuous lectionary which systematically covers the

---

[16] Davis, *Sacred Roots*, (TUMI: 2010), 104.
[17] For more information on the church year see *Understanding the Church Year: A Guide to Colors, Themes, and History* (Appendix 7, pp. 157–65).

Scriptures, and does not attempt to coordinate the texts by a theme. For this reason, the Kingdomtide lectionary topics may apply only to the Gospel text. A leader is free to emphasize another topic if desired, especially during Kingdomtide. The topic given need not always determine the theme of a given Sunday service, or the topic of the sermon.

We have also included a weekly prayer. This prayer is adapted from the Book of Common Prayer's weekly thematic prayers for the church year.[18] In addition, we have provided a brief weekly passage for meditation/memorization. This passage is drawn from that week's lectionary and relates to the theme of the season. In choosing the passages, we have consulted the *Master the Bible* system of verse memorization.[19] *Master the Bible* gives a comprehensive and thematic look at scripture. Following their lead, we have chosen key biblical texts that cover a wide range of important themes.

---

[18] The prayers are adaptations of the Contemporary Collects from *The Book of Common Prayer*, 1979 Ed.

[19] Don L. Davis, *Master the Bible Guidebook*, TUMI, 2008.

THE CHURCH YEAR GUIDE

The Church Year At-A-Glance

Adapted from *Look Back, Look Around, Look Ahead: The Church Year At-A-Glance* by Dr. Don L. Davis, TUMI.

Advent, Christmas, Epiphany: The Cycle of Light

Advent Season: The Coming of Christ (Isaiah 9.6–7)

Advent invites the church both to recall the days prior to the first coming of Christ and to anticipate with hope the second coming of Christ.

- ❖ 1st Sunday of Advent: *Anticipation*

- ❖ 2nd Sunday of Advent: *Annunciation*

- ❖ 3rd Sunday of Advent: *Affirmation*

- ❖ 4th Sunday of Advent: *Arrival*

Christmas Season: The Birth of Christ (John 1.14)

Christmas invites the church to celebrate the incarnation of God the Son, born of the virgin Mary, and to allow Christ to become incarnate in our hearts.

- ❖ Christmas Day (December 25): *The Nativity of Our Lord*

- ❖ 1st Sunday After Christmas

- ❖ 2nd Sunday After Christmas[20]

---

[20] Some years will not contain the Second Sunday after *Christmas*. On years where this second Sunday does occur, you can always choose to celebrate the *Epiphany* on this Sunday (see p. 72 for the lectionary texts for the *Epiphany*).

Epiphany Season: The Manifestation of Christ (Matthew 17.5)

The Epiphany invites the church to affirm that in Jesus of Nazareth the kingdom of God is shining its light into the dark realm of the devil.

- ❖ The Epiphany (January 6): *The Appearing of Our Lord*
- ❖ 1st Sunday After Epiphany: *The Baptism of Our Lord*
- ❖ 2nd– 8th Sunday After Epiphany[21]
- ❖ Last Sunday After Epiphany: *The Transfiguration of Our Lord*

Lent, Easter, Pentecost: The Cycle of Life

Lenten Season (Lent): The Lowliness of Christ (1 John 3.8)

Lent invites the church to take up the cross and walk with Christ the path of complete humility and servanthood.

- ❖ Ash Wednesday
- ❖ 1st Sunday in Lent: *The Temptation of Our Lord*
- ❖ 2nd– 5th Sundays in Lent

Holy Week: The Suffering and Death of Christ (Mark 10.45)

Holy Week invites the church to suffer and die with our Lord that we may be raised to new life with him.

The Great Three Days (Paschal Triduum)

- ❖ Maundy Thursday: *The Giving of the New Commandment*
- ❖ Good Friday: *The Crucifixion and Burial of Our Lord*
- ❖ Holy Saturday

---

[21] The number of Sundays in *Epiphany* varies depending on the date of *Easter* in the particular calendar year.

Easter Season: The Resurrection of Christ (Mark 16.6)

Easter invites the church to shout for joy because Jesus is risen from the dead and seated at the right hand of the Father; Christ is the victor over sin, death, and Satan!

- ❖ Easter Sunday: The Resurrection of Our Lord

- ❖ 2nd– 6th Sundays of Easter

- ❖ Ascension Sunday (7th Sunday of Easter)

- ❖ Pentecost: The Coming of the Holy Spirit

Kingdomtide (Ordinary Time)

A Season of Christ's Headship, Harvest, and Hope (Matthew 28.18–20)

Kingdomtide invites the Spirit-filled church to submit to the headship of Christ our Lord, to labor for the harvest of Christ our Savior, and to anticipate with hope the second coming of Christ our King.

- ❖ 1st Sunday After Pentecost: *Trinity Sunday*

- ❖ 2nd – 27th Sundays After Pentecost (Numbered Propers)[22]

- ❖ All Saints Day (Sunday Closest to November 1)

- ❖ Last Sunday of the Church Year: *The Reign of Christ the King*

---

[22] The number of Sundays in Kingdomtide varies depending on the date of *Easter* in the particular calendar year.

Specific Details for Church Years 2014–24

Year	A,B,C	Advent: Week 1	Weeks of Christmas	Weeks in Epiphany†	Ash Wed.	Easter	Trinity Sunday	First Proper
2014–15	B	11/30/14	2	7	2/18/15	4/5/15	5/31/15	5
2015–16	C	11/29/15	2	5	2/10/16	3/27/16	5/22/16	4
2016–17	A	11/27/16	2*	8	3/1/17	4/16/17	6/11/17	6
2017–18	B	12/3/17	1	6	2/14/18	4/1/18	5/27/18	4
2018–19	C	12/2/18	1♦	9	3/6/19	4/21/19	6/16/19	7
2019–20	A	12/1/19	2	7	2/26/20	4/12/20	6/7/20	6
2020–21	B	11/29/20	2	6	2/17/21	4/4/21	5/30/21	5
2021–22	C	11/28/21	2	8	3/2/22	4/17/22	6/12/22	7
2022–23	A	11/27/22	2*	7	2/22/23	4/9/23	6/4/23	5
2023–24	B	12/3/23	1	6	2/14/24	3/31/24	5/26/24	4

---

† Including *Transfiguration Sunday*, which is always the last Sunday of *Epiphany*.

* *Christmas Day* falls on Sunday. The following Sunday uses *Christmas: Week 1*. *Christmas: Week 2* is not used.

♦ *The Epiphany* (1/6) falls on a Sunday and marks the beginning of the season of *Epiphany*. *Christmas: Week 2* is not used.

Specific Details for Church Years 2024–34

Year	A,B,C	Advent: Week 1	Weeks of Christmas	Weeks in Epiphany†	Ash Wed.	Easter	Trinity Sunday	First Proper
2024–25	C	12/1/24	2	8	3/5/25	4/20/25	6/15/25	7
2025–26	A	11/30/25	2	6	2/18/26	4/5/26	5/31/26	5
2026–27	B	11/29/26	2	5	2/10/27	3/28/27	5/23/27	4
2027–28	C	11/28/27	2	8	3/2/28	4/16/28	6/11/28	6
2028–29	A	12/3/28	1	6	2/14/29	4/1/29	5/27/29	4
2029–30	B	12/2/29	1♦	9	3/6/30	4/21/30	6/16/30	7
2030–31	C	12/1/30	1	7	2/26/31	4/13/31	6/8/31	6
2031–32	A	11/30/31	2	5	2/11/32	3/28/32	5/23/32	4
2032–33	B	11/28/32	2	8	3/2/33	4/17/33	6/12/33	7
2033–34	C	11/27/33	2*	7	2/22/34	4/9/34	6/4/34	5

† Including *Transfiguration Sunday*, which is always the last Sunday of *Epiphany*.
♦ *The Epiphany* (1/6) falls on a Sunday and marks the beginning of the season of *Epiphany*. *Christmas: Week 2* is not used.
* *Christmas Day* falls on Sunday. The following Sunday uses *Christmas: Week 1*. *Christmas: Week 2* is not used.

ADVENT: WEEK 1
The Coming of Christ

Color: Purple
Royalty, Repentance

Prayer: Almighty God, give us grace to cast away the works of darkness, and put on the armor of light, as we remember how your Son Jesus Christ came to us in great humility; that in the last day, when he shall come again in his glorious majesty to judge both the living and the dead, we may rise to the life immortal; through him who lives and reigns with you and the Holy Spirit, one God, now and forever. Amen.

YEAR **A**	**Lectionary Topic:** *Anticipation* **Texts:** Isaiah 2.1–5 Psalm 122 Matthew 24.36–44 Romans 13.11–14 **Passage for Memorization/Meditation:** Romans 13.12
YEAR **B**	**Lectionary Topic:** *Anticipation* **Texts:** Isaiah 64.1–9 Psalm 80.1–7, 17–19 Mark 13.24–37 1 Corinthians 1.3–9 **Passage for Memorization/Meditation:** Mark 13.31
YEAR **C**	**Lectionary Topic:** *Anticipation* **Texts:** Jeremiah 33.14–16 Psalm 25.1–10 Luke 21.25–36 1 Thessalonians 3.9–13 **Passage for Memorization/Meditation:** Jeremiah 33.15

ADVENT: WEEK 2
The Coming of Christ

Color: Purple
Royalty, Repentance

Prayer: Merciful God, who sent your messengers the prophets to preach repentance and prepare the way for our salvation: Give us grace to heed their warnings and forsake our sins, that we may greet with joy the coming of Jesus Christ our Redeemer; who lives and reigns with you and the Holy Spirit, one God, now and forever. Amen.

YEAR **A**	**Lectionary Topic:** *Annunciation* **Texts:** Isaiah 11.1–10 Psalm 72.1–7, 18–19 Matthew 3.1–12 Romans 15.4–13 **Passage for Memorization/Meditation:** Isaiah 11.1–2
YEAR **B**	**Lectionary Topic:** *Annunciation* **Texts:** Isaiah 40.1–11 Psalm 85.1–2, 8–13 Mark 1.1–8 2 Peter 3.8–15a **Passage for Memorization/Meditation:** Mark 1.7–8
YEAR **C**	**Lectionary Topic:** *Annunciation* **Texts:** Malachi 3.1–4 *Luke 1.68–79 (Psalm for the Week)* Luke 3.1–6 Philippians 1.3–11 **Passage for Memorization/Meditation:** Luke 1.68–69

ADVENT: WEEK 3
The Coming of Christ

Color: Rose
Joy, Happiness

Prayer: Stir up your power, O Lord, and with great might come among us; and, because we are sorely hindered by our sins, let your bountiful grace and mercy come to help and deliver us; through Jesus Christ our Lord, to whom, with you and the Holy Spirit, be honor and glory, now and forever. Amen.

YEAR **A**	**Lectionary Topic:** *Affirmation* **Texts:** Isaiah 35.1–10 Psalm 146.5–10 Matthew 11.2–11 James 5.7–10 **Passage for Memorization/Meditation:** Matthew 11.4–6
YEAR **B**	**Lectionary Topic:** *Affirmation* **Texts:** Isaiah 61.1–4, 8–11 Psalm 126 John 1.6–8, 19–28 1 Thessalonians 5.16–24 **Passage for Memorization/Meditation:** John 1.23
YEAR **C**	**Lectionary Topic:** *Affirmation* **Texts:** Zephaniah 3.14–20 *Isaiah 12.2–6 (Psalm for the Week)* Luke 3.7–18 Philippians 4.4–7 **Passage for Memorization/Meditation:** Isaiah 12.3–4

ADVENT: WEEK 4
The Coming of Christ

Color: Purple
Royalty, Repentance

Prayer: Purify our conscience, Almighty God, by your daily visitation, that your Son Jesus Christ, at his coming, may find in us a holy dwelling prepared for himself; who lives and reigns with you, in the unity of the Holy Spirit, one God, now and forever. Amen.

YEAR A	**Lectionary Topic:** *Arrival* **Texts:** Isaiah 7.10–16 Psalm 80.1–7, 17–19 Matthew 1.18–25 Romans 1.1–7 **Passage for Memorization/Meditation:** Isaiah 7.14
YEAR B	**Lectionary Topic:** *Arrival* **Texts:** 2 Samuel 7.1–16 *Luke 1.46b–55 (Psalm for the Week)* Luke 1.26–38 Romans 16.25–27 **Passage for Memorization/Meditation:** Luke 1.31–33
YEAR C	**Lectionary Topic:** *Arrival* **Texts:** Micah 5.2–5a *Luke 1.46b–55 (Psalm for the Week)* Luke 1.39–45 [46–55] Hebrews 10.5–10 **Passage for Memorization/Meditation:** Luke 1.46–48

CHRISTMAS DAY
The Birth of Christ

Color: Gold
Light, Presence of God

Prayer: Almighty God, you have given your only begotten Son to take our nature upon him, and to be born this day of a pure virgin: Grant that we, who have been born again and made your children by adoption and grace, may daily be renewed by your Holy Spirit; through our Lord Jesus Christ, to whom with you and the same Spirit be honor and glory, now and forever. Amen.

YEARS A, B, & C

Texts: Isaiah 9.2–7
Psalm 96
Luke 2.1–20
Titus 2.11–14

CHRISTMAS: WEEK 1
The Birth of Christ

Color: Gold
Light, Presence of God

Prayer: Almighty God, you have poured upon us the new light of your incarnate Word: Grant that this light, enkindled in our hearts, may shine forth in our lives; through Jesus Christ our Lord, who lives and reigns with you, in the unity of the Holy Spirit, one God, now and forever. Amen.

YEAR **A**	**Lectionary Topic:** *Incarnation* **Texts:** Isaiah 63.7–9 Psalm 148 Matthew 2.13–23 Hebrews 2.10–18 **Passage for Memorization/Meditation:** Hebrews 2.14–15
YEAR **B**	**Lectionary Topic:** *Incarnation* **Texts:** Isaiah 61.10—62.3 Psalm 148 Luke 2.22–40 Galatians 4.4–7 **Passage for Memorization/Meditation:** Luke 2.10–11 (*From Christmas Day Readings*)
YEAR **C**	**Lectionary Topic:** *Incarnation* **Texts:** 1 Samuel 2.18–20, 26 Psalm 148 Luke 2.41–52 Colossians 3.12–17 **Passage for Memorization/Meditation:** Isaiah 9.6–7 (*From Christmas Day Readings*)

CHRISTMAS: WEEK 2
The Birth of Christ

Color: Gold
Light, Presence of God

Prayer: O God, who wonderfully created, and yet more wonderfully restored, the dignity of human nature: Grant that we may share the divine life of him who humbled himself to share our humanity, your Son Jesus Christ; who lives and reigns with you, in the unity of the Holy Spirit, one God, forever and ever. Amen.

YEAR **A**	**Lectionary Topic:** *Redemption in God's Grace* **Texts:** Jeremiah 31.7–14 Psalm 147.12–20 John 1.1–18 Ephesians 1.3–14 **Passage for Memorization/Meditation:** John 1.12–13
YEAR **B**	**Lectionary Topic:** *Redemption in God's Grace* **Texts:** Jeremiah 31.7–14 Psalm 147.12–20 John 1.1–18 Ephesians 1.3–14 **Passage for Memorization/Meditation:** John 1.14
YEAR **C**	**Lectionary Topic:** *Redemption in God's Grace* **Texts:** Jeremiah 31.7–14 Psalm 147.12–20 John 1.1–18 Ephesians 1.3–14 **Passage for Memorization/Meditation:** John 1.18

THE EPIPHANY (JANUARY 6)

Color: Gold

The Appearing of Our Lord

Light, Presence of God

Prayer: O God, by the leading of a star you manifested your only Son to the peoples of the earth: Lead us, who know you now by faith, to your presence, where we may see your glory face to face; through Jesus Christ our Lord, who lives and reigns with you and the Holy Spirit, one God, now and forever. Amen.

YEARS A, B, & C

Texts: Isaiah 60.1–6
Psalm 72.1–7, 10–14
Matthew 2.1–12
Ephesians 3.1–12

EPIPHANY: WEEK 1
The Manifestation of Christ

Color: Gold
Light, Presence of God

Prayer: Father in heaven, who at the baptism of Jesus in the River Jordan proclaimed him your beloved Son and anointed him with the Holy Spirit: Grant that all who are baptized into his Name may keep the covenant they have made, and boldly confess him as Lord and Savior; who with you and the Holy Spirit lives and reigns, one God, in glory everlasting. Amen.

YEAR **A**	**Lectionary Topic:** *The Baptism of Our Lord* **Texts:** Isaiah 42.1–9 Psalm 29 Matthew 3.13–17 Acts 10.34–43 **Passage for Memorization/Meditation:** Matthew 3.16–17
YEAR **B**	**Lectionary Topic:** *The Baptism of Our Lord* **Texts:** Genesis 1.1–5 Psalm 29 Mark 1.4–11 Acts 19.1–7 **Passage for Memorization/Meditation:** Acts 19.4–5
YEAR **C**	**Lectionary Topic:** *The Baptism of Our Lord* **Texts:** Isaiah 43.1–7 Psalm 29 Luke 3.15–17, 21–22 Acts 8.14–17 **Passage for Memorization/Meditation:** Isaiah 43.1–2

EPIPHANY: WEEK 2
The Manifestation of Christ

Color: Green
Renewal, New Life

Prayer: Almighty God, whose Son our Savior Jesus Christ is the light of the world: Grant that your people, illumined by your Word and Sacraments, may shine with the radiance of Christ's glory, that he may be known, worshiped, and obeyed to the ends of the earth; through Jesus Christ our Lord, who with you and the Holy Spirit lives and reigns, one God, now and forever. Amen.

YEAR **A**	**Lectionary Topic:** *Behold, The Lamb of God* **Texts:** Isaiah 49.1–7 Psalm 40.1–11 John 1.29–42 1 Corinthians 1.1–9 **Passage for Memorization/Meditation:** Isaiah 49.6
YEAR **B**	**Lectionary Topic:** *The Son of God* **Texts:** 1 Samuel 3.1–20 Psalm 139.1–6, 13–18 John 1.43–51 1 Corinthians 6.12–20 **Passage for Memorization/Meditation:** John 1.45
YEAR **C**	**Lectionary Topic:** *Christ's Glory Manifested* **Texts:** Isaiah 62.1–5 Psalm 36.5–10 John 2.1–11 1 Corinthians 12.1–11 **Passage for Memorization/Meditation:** Isaiah 62.2

EPIPHANY: WEEK 3
The Manifestation of Christ

Color: Green
Renewal, New Life

Prayer: Give us grace, O Lord, to answer readily the call of our Savior Jesus Christ and proclaim to all people the Good News of his salvation, that we and the whole world may recognize the glory of his marvelous works; who lives and reigns with you and the Holy Spirit, one God, forever and ever. Amen.

YEAR **A**	**Lectionary Topic:** *A Great Light in the Darkness* **Texts:** Isaiah 9.1–4 Psalm 27.1, 4–9 Matthew 4.12–23 1 Corinthians 1.10–18 **Passage for Memorization/Meditation:** Isaiah 9.2
YEAR **B**	**Lectionary Topic:** *The Kingdom of God is at Hand* **Texts:** Jonah 3.1–5, 10 Psalm 62.5–12 Mark 1.14–20 1 Corinthians 7.29–31 **Passage for Memorization/Meditation:** Mark 1.14–15
YEAR **C**	**Lectionary Topic:** *The Spirit of the Lord is Upon Me* **Texts:** Nehemiah 8.1–10 Psalm 19 Luke 4.14–21 1 Corinthians 12.12–31a **Passage for Memorization/Meditation:** Luke 4.18–19

EPIPHANY: WEEK 4
The Manifestation of Christ

Color: Green
Renewal, New Life

Prayer: Almighty and everlasting God, you govern all things both in heaven and on earth: Mercifully hear the supplications of your people, and in your time grant us your peace; through Jesus Christ our Lord, who lives and reigns with you and the Holy Spirit, one God, forever and ever. Amen.

YEAR **A**	**Lectionary Topic:** *Blessed Are the Poor in Spirit* **Texts:** Micah 6.1–8 Psalm 15 Matthew 5.1–12 1 Corinthians 1.18–31 **Passage for Memorization/Meditation:** Micah 6.8
YEAR **B**	**Lectionary Topic:** *Christ's Authority* **Texts:** Deuteronomy 18.15–20 Psalm 111 Mark 1.21–28 1 Corinthians 8.1–13 **Passage for Memorization/Meditation:** Deuteronomy 18.18
YEAR **C**	**Lectionary Topic:** *Rejection of the Lord* **Texts:** Jeremiah 1.4–10 Psalm 71.1–6 Luke 4.21–30 1 Corinthians 13 **Passage for Memorization/Meditation:** Jeremiah 1.9–10

EPIPHANY: WEEK 5
The Manifestation of Christ

Color: Green
Renewal, New Life

Prayer: Set us free, O God, from the bondage of our sins, and give us the liberty of that abundant life which you have made known to us in your Son our Savior Jesus Christ; who lives and reigns with you, in the unity of the Holy Spirit, one God, now and forever. Amen.

YEAR **A**	**Lectionary Topic:** *Let Your Light Shine* **Texts:** Isaiah 58.1–12 Psalm 112.1–10 Matthew 5.13–20 1 Corinthians 2.1–16 **Passage for Memorization/Meditation:** Matthew 5.16
YEAR **B**	**Lectionary Topic:** *The Preaching and Power of Christ* **Texts:** Isaiah 40.21–31 Psalm 147.1–11, 20c Mark 1.29–39 1 Corinthians 9.16–23 **Passage for Memorization/Meditation:** 1 Corinthians 9.22–23
YEAR **C**	**Lectionary Topic:** *Leaving Everything to Follow Him* **Texts:** Isaiah 6.1–13 Psalm 138 Luke 5.1–11 1 Corinthians 15.1–11 **Passage for Memorization/Meditation:** 1 Corinthians 15.3–5

EPIPHANY: WEEK 6
The Manifestation of Christ

Color: Green
Renewal, New Life

Prayer: O God, the strength of all who put their trust in you: Mercifully accept our prayers; and because in our weakness we can do nothing good without you, give us the help of your grace, that in keeping your commandments we may please you both in will and deed; through Jesus Christ our Lord, who lives and reigns with you and the Holy Spirit, one God, for ever and ever. Amen.

YEAR A	**Lectionary Topic:** *The Law of Christ* **Texts:** Deuteronomy 30.15–20 Psalm 119.1–8 Matthew 5.21–37 1 Corinthians 3.1–9 **Passage for Memorization/Meditation:** Deuteronomy 30.19–20
YEAR B	**Lectionary Topic:** *Made Clean by Christ* **Texts:** 2 Kings 5.1–14 Psalm 30 Mark 1.40–45 1 Corinthians 9.24–27 **Passage for Memorization/Meditation:** Psalm 30.11–12
YEAR C	**Lectionary Topic:** *Blessed Are the Poor* **Texts:** Jeremiah 17.5–10 Psalm 1 Luke 6.17–26 1 Corinthians 15.12–20 **Passage for Memorization/Meditation:** Luke 6.20

EPIPHANY: WEEK 7
The Manifestation of Christ

Color: Green
Renewal, New Life

Prayer: O Lord, you have taught us that without love whatever we do is worthless: Send your Holy Spirit and pour into our hearts your great love, the true bond of peace and of all virtue, without which we are hopeless. Grant this for the sake of your only Son Jesus Christ, who lives and reigns with you and the Holy Spirit, one God, now and forever. Amen.

YEAR A	**Lectionary Topic:** *Love Your Enemies* **Texts:** Leviticus 19.1–18 Psalm 119.33–40 Matthew 5.38–48 1 Corinthians 3.10–23 **Passage for Memorization/Meditation:** Leviticus 19.18
YEAR B	**Lectionary Topic:** *Forgiveness of Sins in Christ* **Texts:** Isaiah 43.18–25 Psalm 41 Mark 2.1–12 2 Corinthians 1.18–22 **Passage for Memorization/Meditation:** 2 Corinthians 1.19–20
YEAR C	**Lectionary Topic:** *Be Merciful as Your Father is Merciful* **Texts:** Genesis 45.3–15 Psalm 37.1–11, 39–40 Luke 6.27–38 1 Corinthians 15.35–50 **Passage for Memorization/Meditation:** Luke 6.35

EPIPHANY: WEEK 8
The Manifestation of Christ

Color: Green
Renewal, New Life

Prayer: Most loving Father, whose will it is for us to give thanks for all things, and to cast all our care on you who cares for us: Preserve us from faithless fears and worldly anxieties, that no clouds of this mortal life may hide from us the light of that love which is immortal, and which you have manifested to us in your Son Jesus Christ our Lord; who lives and reigns with you, in the unity of the Holy Spirit, one God, now and forever. Amen.

YEAR **A**	**Lectionary Topic:** *Seek First the Kingdom of God* **Texts:** Isaiah 49.8–16 Psalm 131 Matthew 6.24–34 1 Corinthians 4.1–5 **Passage for Memorization/Meditation:** Matthew 6.33
YEAR **B**	**Lectionary Topic:** *Christ Calls Sinners* **Texts:** Hosea 2.14–20 Psalm 103.1–13, 22 Mark 2.13–22 2 Corinthians 3.1–6 **Passage for Memorization/Meditation:** Mark 2.17
YEAR **C**	**Lectionary Topic:** *Founded on the Rock* **Texts:** Isaiah 55.10–13 Psalm 92.1–4, 12–15 Luke 6.39–49 1 Corinthians 15.51–58 **Passage for Memorization/Meditation:** Isaiah 55.11

EPIPHANY: LAST WEEK
The Manifestation of Christ

Color: Gold
Light, Presence of God

Prayer: O God, who before the passion of your only begotten Son revealed his glory upon the holy mountain: Grant to us that we, beholding by faith the light of his countenance, may be strengthened to bear our cross, and be changed into his likeness from glory to glory; through Jesus Christ our Lord, who lives and reigns with you and the Holy Spirit, one God, forever and ever. Amen.

YEAR **A**	**Lectionary Topic:** *The Transfiguration of Our Lord* **Texts:** Exodus 24.12–18 Psalm 2 Matthew 17.1–9 2 Peter 1.16–21 **Passage for Memorization/Meditation:** Matthew 17.5
YEAR **B**	**Lectionary Topic:** *The Transfiguration of Our Lord* **Texts:** 2 Kings 2.1–12 Psalm 50.1–6 Mark 9.2–9 2 Corinthians 4.3–6 **Passage for Memorization/Meditation:** 2 Corinthians 4.5–6
YEAR **C**	**Lectionary Topic:** *The Transfiguration of Our Lord* **Texts:** Exodus 34.29–35 Psalm 99 Luke 9.28–36 2 Corinthians 3.12 — 4.2 **Passage for Memorization/Meditation:** 2 Corinthians 3.18

ASH WEDNESDAY
The Lowliness of Christ
(Beginning of Lent)

Color: Purple
Royalty, Repentance

Prayer: Almighty and everlasting God, you hate nothing you have made and forgive the sins of all who repent: Create and make in us new and contrite hearts, that we, truly lamenting our sins and acknowledging our wretchedness, may obtain of you, the God of all mercy, perfect remission and forgiveness; through Jesus Christ our Lord, who lives and reigns with you and the Holy Spirit, one God, forever and ever. Amen.

YEARS A, B, & C

Texts: Joel 2.1–2, 12–17
Psalm 51.1–17
Matthew 6.1–6, 16–21
2 Corinthians 5.20 — 6.10

LENT: WEEK 1
The Lowliness of Christ

Color: Purple
Royalty, Repentance

Prayer: Almighty God, whose blessed Son was led by the Spirit to be tempted by Satan: Come quickly to help us who are assaulted by many temptations; and, as you know the weaknesses of each of us, let each one find you mighty to save; through Jesus Christ your Son our Lord, who lives and reigns with you and the Holy Spirit, one God, now and forever. Amen.

YEAR **A**	**Lectionary Topic:** *The Temptation of Our Lord* **Texts:** Genesis 2.15–17; 3.1–7 Psalm 32 Matthew 4.1–11 Romans 5.12–19 **Passage for Memorization/Meditation:** Matthew 4.1
YEAR **B**	**Lectionary Topic:** *The Temptation of Our Lord* **Texts:** Genesis 9.8–17 Psalm 25.1–10 Mark 1.9–15 1 Peter 3.18–22 **Passage for Memorization/Meditation:** 1 Peter 3.18
YEAR **C**	**Lectionary Topic:** *The Temptation of Our Lord* **Texts:** Deuteronomy 26.1–11 Psalm 91.1–2, 9–16 Luke 4.1–13 Romans 10.8–13 **Passage for Memorization/Meditation:** Psalm 91.13

LENT: WEEK 2
The Lowliness of Christ

Color: Purple
Royalty, Repentance

Prayer: O God, whose glory it is always to have mercy: Be gracious to all who have gone astray from your ways, and bring them again with repentant hearts and steadfast faith to embrace and hold fast the unchangeable truth of your Word, Jesus Christ your Son; who with you and the Holy Spirit lives and reigns, one God, for ever and ever. Amen.

YEAR A	**Lectionary Topic:** *Eternal Life by Faith in Christ* **Texts:** Genesis 12.1–4 Psalm 121 John 3.1–17 Romans 4.1–5, 13–17 **Passage for Memorization/Meditation:** John 3.16–17
YEAR B	**Lectionary Topic:** *Take Up Your Cross* **Texts:** Genesis 17.1–7, 15–16 Psalm 22.23–31 Mark 8.31–38 Romans 4.13–25 **Passage for Memorization/Meditation:** Mark 8.34
YEAR C	**Lectionary Topic:** *Christ Rejected by God's People* **Texts:** Genesis 15.1–12, 17–18 Psalm 27 Luke 13.31–35 Philippians 3.17 – 4.1 **Passage for Memorization/Meditation:** Psalm 27.1

LENT: WEEK 3
The Lowliness of Christ

Color: Purple
Royalty, Repentance

Prayer: Almighty God, you know that we have no power in ourselves to help ourselves: Keep us both outwardly in our bodies and inwardly in our souls, that we may be defended from the enemy, who would attack our bodies and assault our souls; through Jesus Christ our Lord, who lives and reigns with you and the Holy Spirit, one God, forever and ever. Amen.

YEAR **A**	**Lectionary Topic:** *The Water Christ Gives* **Texts:** Exodus 17.1–7 Psalm 95 John 4.5–42 Romans 5.1–11 **Passage for Memorization/Meditation:** John 4.13–14
YEAR **B**	**Lectionary Topic:** *Christ's Zeal for God's House* **Texts:** Exodus 20.1–17 Psalm 19 John 2.13–22 1 Corinthians 1.18–25 **Passage for Memorization/Meditation:** 1 Corinthians 1.18
YEAR **C**	**Lectionary Topic:** *Repent or Perish* **Texts:** Isaiah 55.1–9 Psalm 63.1–8 Luke 13.1–9 1 Corinthians 10.1–13 **Passage for Memorization/Meditation:** 1 Corinthians 10.11–12

LENT: WEEK 4
The Lowliness of Christ

Color: Purple
Royalty, Repentance

Prayer: Gracious Father, whose blessed Son Jesus Christ came down from heaven to be the true bread which gives life to the world: Evermore give us this bread, that he may live in us, and we in him; who lives and reigns with you and the Holy Spirit, one God, now and forever. Amen.

YEAR **A**	**Lectionary Topic:** *Sight for the Blind* **Texts:** 1 Samuel 16.1–13 Psalm 23 John 9.1–41 Ephesians 5.8–14 **Passage for Memorization/Meditation:** Ephesians 5.8–9
YEAR **B**	**Lectionary Topic:** *Light in the Darkness* **Texts:** Numbers 21.4–9 Psalm 107.1–3, 17–22 John 3.14–21 Ephesians 2.1–10 **Passage for Memorization/Meditation:** John 3.19
YEAR **C**	**Lectionary Topic:** *What Was Lost Is Found* **Texts:** Joshua 5.9–12 Psalm 32 Luke 15.1–32 2 Corinthians 5.16–21 **Passage for Memorization/Meditation:** 2 Corinthians 5.17–18

LENT: WEEK 5
The Lowliness of Christ

Color: Purple
Royalty, Repentance

Prayer: Almighty God, you alone can bring into order the unruly wills and affections of sinners: Grant your people grace to love what you command and desire what you promise; that, among the constant changes of the world, our hearts may surely there be fixed where true joys are to be found; through Jesus Christ our Lord, who lives and reigns with you and the Holy Spirit, one God, now and forever. Amen.

YEAR **A**	**Lectionary Topic:** *Life for the Dead* **Texts:** Ezekiel 37.1–14 Psalm 130 John 11.1–45 Romans 8.6–11 **Passage for Memorization/Meditation:** John 11.25
YEAR **B**	**Lectionary Topic:** *The Ruler of This World Cast Out* **Texts:** Jeremiah 31.31–34 Psalm 51.1–12 John 12.20–33 Hebrews 5.5–10 **Passage for Memorization/Meditation:** John 12.31–32
YEAR **C**	**Lectionary Topic:** *Mary Anoints Jesus* **Texts:** Isaiah 43.16–21 Psalm 126 John 12.1–8 Philippians 3.4–14 **Passage for Memorization/Meditation:** Philippians 3.7–8

HOLY WEEK: PALM SUNDAY
The Triumphal Entry

Color: Purple
Royalty, Repentance

Prayer: Almighty and eternal God, in your tender love for humanity you sent your Son our Savior Jesus Christ to take upon him our nature, and to suffer death upon the cross, giving us the example of his great humility: Mercifully grant that we may walk in the way of his suffering, and also share in his resurrection; through Jesus Christ our Lord, who lives and reigns with you and the Holy Spirit, one God, forever and ever. Amen.

YEAR A	**Lectionary Topic:** *The Triumphal Entry* **Texts:** Isaiah 50.4–9 Psalm 31.9–16 Matthew 21.1–11 Philippians 2.5–11 **Passage for Memorization/Meditation:** Matthew 21.9
YEAR B	**Lectionary Topic:** *The Triumphal Entry* **Texts:** Isaiah 50.4–9 Psalm 31.9–16 Mark 11.1–11 Philippians 2.5–11 **Passage for Memorization/Meditation:** Philippians 2.6–8
YEAR C	**Lectionary Topic:** *The Triumphal Entry* **Texts:** Isaiah 50.4–9a Psalm 31.9–16 Luke 19.28–40 Philippians 2.5–11 **Passage for Memorization/Meditation:** Philippians 2.9–11

HOLY WEEK:
MAUNDY THURSDAY

The Giving of the New Commandment

*Color: **Purple***
Royalty, Repentance

Prayer: Almighty Father, whose dear Son, on the night before he suffered, instituted the Sacrament of his Body and Blood: Mercifully grant that we may receive it thankfully in remembrance of Jesus Christ our Lord, who in these holy mysteries gives us a pledge of eternal life; and who now lives and reigns with you and the Holy Spirit, one God, forever and ever. Amen.

YEARS A, B, & C

Texts: Exodus 12.1–14
Psalm 116.1–2, 12–19
John 13.1–17, 31–35
1 Corinthians 11.23–26

HOLY WEEK: GOOD FRIDAY

The Crucifixion and Burial of Our Lord

Color: Purple
Royalty, Repentance

Prayer: Almighty God, we pray you look on your children with grace, for whom our Lord Jesus Christ was willing to be betrayed, and given into the hands of sinners, and to suffer death upon the cross; who now lives and reigns with you and the Holy Spirit, one God, forever and ever. Amen.

YEARS A, B, & C

Texts: Isaiah 52.13—53.12
Psalm 22
John 18.1—19.42
Hebrews 10.16–25

HOLY WEEK:
HOLY SATURDAY

Prayer: O God, Creator of heaven and earth: Grant that, as the crucified body of your dear Son was laid in the tomb and rested on this holy Sabbath, so we may await with him the coming of the third day, and rise with him to newness of life; who now lives and reigns with you and the Holy Spirit, one God, forever and ever. Amen.

YEARS A, B, & C

Texts: Job 14.1–14
Psalm 31.1–4, 15–16
John 19.38–42
1 Peter 4.1–8

EASTER SUNDAY
The Resurrection of Our Lord

Color: Gold
Light, Presence of God

Prayer: O God, who for our redemption gave your only begotten Son to the death of the cross, and by his glorious resurrection delivered us from the power of our enemy: Grant us so to die daily to sin, that we may live with him in the joy and victory of his resurrection; through Jesus Christ your Son our Lord, who lives and reigns with you and the Holy Spirit, one God, now and forever. Amen.

YEAR **A**	**Lectionary Topic:** *The Resurrection of Our Lord* **Texts:** Jeremiah 31.1–6 Psalm 118.1–2, 14–24 Matthew 28.1–10 Colossians 3.1–4 **Passage for Memorization/Meditation:** Acts 10.38–40
YEAR **B**	**Lectionary Topic:** *The Resurrection of Our Lord* **Texts:** Isaiah 25.6–9 Psalm 118.1–2, 14–24 Mark 16.1–8 1 Corinthians 15.1–11 **Passage for Memorization/Meditation:** Mark 16.6–7
YEAR **C**	**Lectionary Topic:** *The Resurrection of Our Lord* **Texts:** Acts 10.34–43 Psalm 118.1–2, 14–24 Luke 24.1–12 1 Corinthians 15.19–26 **Passage for Memorization/Meditation:** 1 Corinthians 15.19–20

EASTER: WEEK 2
The Resurrection of Christ

Color: Gold
Light, Presence of God

Prayer: Almighty and everlasting God, who in the resurrection of Jesus established the new covenant of reconciliation: Grant that all who have been reborn into the fellowship of Christ's body may show forth in our lives what we profess by our faith; through Jesus Christ our Lord, who lives and reigns with you and the Holy Spirit, one God, forever and ever. Amen.

YEAR **A**	**Lectionary Topic:** *My Lord and My God* **Texts:** Acts 2.14a, 22–32 Psalm 16 John 20.19–31 1 Peter 1.3–9 **Passage for Memorization/Meditation:** John 20.28–29
YEAR **B**	**Lectionary Topic:** *My Lord and My God* **Texts:** Acts 4.32–35 Psalm 133 John 20.19–31 1 John 1.1—2.2 **Passage for Memorization/Meditation:** 1 John 1.8–9
YEAR **C**	**Lectionary Topic:** *My Lord and My God* **Texts:** Acts 5.27–32 Psalm 150 John 20.19–31 Revelation 1.4–8 **Passage for Memorization/Meditation:** Revelation 1.8

EASTER: WEEK 3
The Resurrection of Christ

Color: Gold
Light, Presence of God

Prayer: O God, whose blessed Son made himself known to his disciples in the breaking of bread: Open the eyes of our faith, that we may behold the risen Lord in all his redeeming work; who lives and reigns with you, in the unity of the Holy Spirit, one God, now and forever. Amen.

YEAR **A**	**Lectionary Topic:** *The Lord Has Risen Indeed* **Texts:** Acts 2.14a, 36–41 Psalm 116.1–4, 12–19 Luke 24.13–35 1 Peter 1.17–23 **Passage for Memorization/Meditation:** Luke 24.26–27
YEAR **B**	**Lectionary Topic:** *Christ Fulfills the Scriptures* **Texts:** Acts 3.12–19 Psalm 4 Luke 24.36–48 1 John 3.1–7 **Passage for Memorization/Meditation:** Luke 24.44
YEAR **C**	**Lectionary Topic:** *Feed My Sheep* **Texts:** Acts 9.1–20 Psalm 30 John 21.1–19 Revelation 5.11–14 **Passage for Memorization/Meditation:** Revelation 5.9–10

EASTER: WEEK 4
The Resurrection of Christ

Color: Gold
Light, Presence of God

Prayer: O God, whose Son Jesus is the good shepherd of your people: Grant that when we hear his voice we may know him who calls us each by name, and follow where he leads; who, with you and the Holy Spirit, lives and reigns, one God, forever and ever. Amen.

YEAR **A**	**Lectionary Topic:** *The Lord Our Shepherd* **Texts:** Acts 2.42–47 Psalm 23 John 10.1–10 1 Peter 2.19–25 **Passage for Memorization/Meditation:** Psalm 23.1–2
YEAR **B**	**Lectionary Topic:** *The Lord Our Shepherd* **Texts:** Acts 4.5–12 Psalm 23 John 10.11–18 1 John 3.16–24 **Passage for Memorization/Meditation:** John 10.14–15
YEAR **C**	**Lectionary Topic:** *The Lord Our Shepherd* **Texts:** Acts 9.36–43 Psalm 23 John 10.22–30 Revelation 7.9–17 **Passage for Memorization/Meditation:** John 10.27–28

EASTER: WEEK 5

The Resurrection of Christ

Color: Gold
Light, Presence of God

Prayer: Almighty God, knowing you is everlasting life. Grant us so perfectly to know your Son Jesus Christ to be the way, the truth, and the life, that we may faithfully follow his steps in the way that leads to eternal life; through Jesus Christ your Son our Lord, who lives and reigns with you, in the unity of the Holy Spirit, one God, forever and ever. Amen.

YEAR **A**	**Lectionary Topic:** *The Way, the Truth, and the Life* **Texts:** Acts 7.55–60 Psalm 31.1–5, 15–16 John 14.1–14 1 Peter 2.2–10 **Passage for Memorization/Meditation:** John 14.6
YEAR **B**	**Lectionary Topic:** *Christ Is the Vine* **Texts:** Acts 8.26–40 Psalm 22.25–31 John 15.1–8 1 John 4.7–21 **Passage for Memorization/Meditation:** John 15.5
YEAR **C**	**Lectionary Topic:** *Love One Another* **Texts:** Acts 11.1–18 Psalm 148 John 13.31–35 Revelation 21.1–6 **Passage for Memorization/Meditation:** John 13.34–35

EASTER: WEEK 6
The Resurrection of Christ

Color: Gold
Light, Presence of God

Prayer: O God, you have prepared for those who love you such good things as surpass our understanding: Pour into our hearts such love towards you, that we, loving you in all things and above all things, may obtain your promises, which exceed all that we can desire; through Jesus Christ our Lord, who lives and reigns with you and the Holy Spirit, one God, forever and ever. Amen.

YEAR A	**Lectionary Topic:** *The Spirit of Truth* **Texts:** Acts 17.22–31 Psalm 66.8–20 John 14.15–21 1 Peter 3.13–22 **Passage for Memorization/Meditation:** John 14.16–17
YEAR B	**Lectionary Topic:** *Friends of Christ* **Texts:** Acts 10.44–48 Psalm 98 John 15.9–17 1 John 5.1–6 **Passage for Memorization/Meditation:** 1 John 5.4–5
YEAR C	**Lectionary Topic:** *God Makes His Home With Us* **Texts:** Acts 16.9–15 Psalm 67 John 14.23–29 Revelation 21.10, 22–22.5 **Passage for Memorization/Meditation:** Revelation 22.3–4

ASCENSION SUNDAY
The Ascension of Our Lord

Color: Gold
Light, Presence of God

Prayer: O God, the King of glory, you have exalted your only Son Jesus Christ with great triumph to your kingdom in heaven: Do not leave us comfortless, but send us your Holy Spirit to strengthen us, and exalt us to that place where our Savior Christ has gone before; who lives and reigns with you and the Holy Spirit, one God, in glory everlasting. Amen.

YEAR A	**Lectionary Topic:** *The Ascension of Our Lord* **Texts:** Acts 1.6–14 Psalm 68.1–10, 32–35 John 17.1–11 1 Peter 4.12–14; 5.6–11 **Passage for Memorization/Meditation:** 1 Peter 5.8–9
YEAR B	**Lectionary Topic:** *The Ascension of Our Lord* **Texts:** Acts 1.1–11 Psalm 1 John 17.6–19 1 John 5.9–13 **Passage for Memorization/Meditation:** 1 John 5.11–12
YEAR C	**Lectionary Topic:** *The Ascension of Our Lord* **Texts:** Acts 1.1–11 Psalm 47 Luke 24.44–53 Ephesians 1.15–23 **Passage for Memorization/Meditation:** Acts 1.8–9

PENTECOST
The Coming of the Holy Spirit

Color: Red
Fire, Blood of Martyrs

Prayer: Almighty God, on this day you opened the way of eternal life to every race and nation by the promised gift of your Holy Spirit: Give this gift throughout the world by the preaching of the Gospel, that all may turn from the darkness to the light, and from the power of Satan to God; through Jesus Christ our Lord, who lives and reigns with you, in the unity of the Holy Spirit, one God, forever and ever. Amen.

YEAR **A**	**Lectionary Topic:** *The Coming of the Holy Spirit* **Texts:** Numbers 11.24–30 Psalm 104.24–34, 35b John 7.37–39 Acts 2.1–21 **Passage for Memorization/Meditation:** Acts 2.2–4
YEAR **B**	**Lectionary Topic:** *The Coming of the Holy Spirit* **Texts:** Ezekiel 37.1–14 Psalm 104.24–34, 35b John 16.4–15 Acts 2.1–21 **Passage for Memorization/Meditation:** Ezekiel 37.13–14
YEAR **C**	**Lectionary Topic:** *The Coming of the Holy Spirit* **Texts:** Acts 2.1–21 Psalm 104.24–34, 35b John 14.8–17 Romans 8.14–17 **Passage for Memorization/Meditation:** Acts 2.16–17

TRINITY SUNDAY
The Triune God

Color: Gold
Light, Presence of God

Prayer: Almighty and everlasting God, you have given to us your servants grace, by the confession of a true faith, to acknowledge the glory of the eternal Trinity, and to worship the one true and living God: Keep us steadfast in this faith and worship, and bring us at last to see you in your one and eternal glory, O Father; who with the Son and the Holy Spirit live and reign, one God, forever and ever. Amen.

YEAR **A**	**Lectionary Topic:** *The Triune God* **Texts:** Genesis 1.1—2.3 Psalm 8 Matthew 28.16–20 2 Corinthians 13.11–13 **Passage for Memorization/Meditation:** Matthew 28.18–20
YEAR **B**	**Lectionary Topic:** *The Triune God* **Texts:** Isaiah 6.1–8 Psalm 29 John 3.1–17 Romans 8.12–17 **Passage for Memorization/Meditation:** Romans 8.15–16
YEAR **C**	**Lectionary Topic:** *The Triune God* **Texts:** Proverbs 8.1–4, 22–31 Psalm 8 John 16.12–15 Romans 5.1–5 **Passage for Memorization/Meditation:** Psalm 8.3–4

KINGDOMTIDE: PROPER 1
The Headship, Harvest, and Hope of Christ

Color: Green
Renewal, New Life

Prayer: Remember, O Lord, what you have formed in us and not what we deserve; and, as you have called us to your service, make us worthy of our calling; through Jesus Christ our Lord, who lives and reigns with you and the Holy Spirit, one God, now and forever. Amen.

YEAR **A**	**Lectionary Topic:** *The Law of Christ* **Texts:** Deuteronomy 30.15–20 Psalm 119.1–8 Matthew 5.21–37 1 Corinthians 3.1–9 **Passage for Memorization/Meditation:** Deuteronomy 30.19–20
YEAR **B**	**Lectionary Topic:** *Made Clean by Christ* **Texts:** 2 Kings 5.1–14 Psalm 30 Mark 1.40–45 1 Corinthians 9.24–27 **Passage for Memorization/Meditation:** Psalm 30.11–12
YEAR **C**	**Lectionary Topic:** *Blessed Are the Poor* **Texts:** Jeremiah 17.5–10 Psalm 1 Luke 6.17–26 1 Corinthians 15.12–20 **Passage for Memorization/Meditation:** Luke 6.20

KINGDOMTIDE: PROPER 2
The Headship, Harvest, and Hope of Christ

Color: Green
Renewal, New Life

Prayer: Almighty and merciful God, in your goodness keep us, we pray, from all the power of the enemy, that we, being ready both in mind and body, may accomplish with free hearts those things which belong to your purpose; through Jesus Christ our Lord, who lives and reigns with you and the Holy Spirit, one God, now and forever. Amen.

YEAR A	**Lectionary Topic:** *Love Your Enemies* **Texts:** Leviticus 19.1–18 Psalm 119.33–40 Matthew 5.38–48 1 Corinthians 3.10–23 **Passage for Memorization/Meditation:** Leviticus 19.18
YEAR B	**Lectionary Topic:** *Forgiveness of Sins in Christ* **Texts:** Isaiah 43.18–25 Psalm 41 Mark 2.1–12 2 Corinthians 1.18–22 **Passage for Memorization/Meditation:** 2 Corinthians 1.19–20
YEAR C	**Lectionary Topic:** *Be Merciful as Your Father is Merciful* **Texts:** Genesis 45.3–15 Psalm 37.1–11, 39–40 Luke 6.27–38 1 Corinthians 15.35–50 **Passage for Memorization/Meditation:** Luke 6.35

KINGDOMTIDE: PROPER 3
The Headship, Harvest, and Hope of Christ

Color: Green
Renewal, New Life

Prayer: Grant, O Lord, that the course of this world may be justly governed by your wisdom; and that your Church may joyfully serve you in confidence and peace; through Jesus Christ our Lord, who lives and reigns with you and the Holy Spirit, one God, forever and ever. Amen.

YEAR A	**Lectionary Topic:** *Seek First the Kingdom of God* **Texts:** Isaiah 49.8–16 Psalm 131 Matthew 6.24–34 1 Corinthians 4.1–5 **Passage for Memorization/Meditation:** Matthew 6.33
YEAR B	**Lectionary Topic:** *Christ Calls Sinners* **Texts:** Hosea 2.14–20 Psalm 103.1–13, 22 Mark 2.13–22 2 Corinthians 3.1–6 **Passage for Memorization/Meditation:** Mark 2.17
YEAR C	**Lectionary Topic:** *Founded on the Rock* **Texts:** Isaiah 55.10–13 Psalm 92.1–4, 12–15 Luke 6.39–49 1 Corinthians 15.51–58 **Passage for Memorization/Meditation:** Isaiah 55.11

KINGDOMTIDE: PROPER 4
The Headship, Harvest, and Hope of Christ

Color: Green
Renewal, New Life

Prayer: O God, your never failing providence sets in order all things both in heaven and earth: Put away from us, we entreat you, all that hinders your will, and give us those things which are truly profitable; through Jesus Christ our Lord, who lives and reigns with you and the Holy Spirit, one God, forever and ever. Amen.

YEAR A	**Lectionary Topic:** *Do the Will of the Father* **Texts:** Genesis 6.9–22; 7.24; 8.14–19 Psalm 46 Matthew 7.21–29 Romans 1.16–17; 3.22–31 **Passage for Memorization/Meditation:** Romans 1.16–17
YEAR B	**Lectionary Topic:** *The Son of Man is Lord* **Texts:** 1 Samuel 3.1–20 Psalm 139.1–6, 13–18 Mark 2.23 — 3.6 2 Corinthians 4.5–12 **Passage for Memorization/Meditation:** 2 Corinthians 4.7–8
YEAR C	**Lectionary Topic:** *The Authority of Christ* **Texts:** 1 Kings 18.20–39 Psalm 96 Luke 7.1–10 Galatians 1.1–12 **Passage for Memorization/Meditation:** 1 Kings 18.21

KINGDOMTIDE: PROPER 5
The Headship, Harvest, and Hope of Christ

Color: Green
Renewal, New Life

Prayer: O God, from whom all good proceeds: Grant that by your inspiration we may think those things that are right, and that by your merciful guiding we may do them; through Jesus Christ our Lord, who lives and reigns with you and the Holy Spirit, one God, forever and ever. Amen.

YEAR **A**	**Lectionary Topic:** *Christ Calls Sinners* **Texts:** Genesis 12.1–9 Psalm 33.1–12 Matthew 9.9–26 Romans 4.13–25 **Passage for Memorization/Meditation:** Genesis 12.2–3
YEAR **B**	**Lectionary Topic:** *The Binding of the Strong Man* **Texts:** 1 Samuel 8.4–15 Psalm 138 Mark 3.20–35 2 Corinthians 4.13—5.1 **Passage for Memorization/Meditation:** 2 Corinthians 4.16–17
YEAR **C**	**Lectionary Topic:** *The Compassionate Life-Giver* **Texts:** 1 Kings 17.8–16 Psalm 146 Luke 7.11–17 Galatians 1.11–24 **Passage for Memorization/Meditation:** Luke 7.16

KINGDOMTIDE: PROPER 6
The Headship, Harvest, and Hope of Christ

Color: Green
Renewal, New Life

Prayer: Keep, O Lord, your household the Church in your steadfast faith and love, that through your grace we may proclaim your truth with boldness, and minister your justice with compassion; for the sake of our Savior Jesus Christ, who lives and reigns with you and the Holy Spirit, one God, now and forever. Amen.

YEAR A	**Lectionary Topic:** *The Harvest Is Plentiful* **Texts:** Genesis 18.1–15 Psalm 116.1–2, 12–19 Matthew 9.35 – 10.8 (9–23) Romans 5.1–8 **Passage for Memorization/Meditation:** Matthew 9.37–38
YEAR B	**Lectionary Topic:** *The Kingdom of God* **Texts:** 1 Samuel 15.34 – 16.13 Psalm 20 Mark 4.26–34 2 Corinthians 5.6–17 **Passage for Memorization/Meditation:** 1 Samuel 16.7
YEAR C	**Lectionary Topic:** *Your Sins Are Forgiven* **Texts:** 1 Kings 21.1–21 Psalm 5.1–8 Luke 7.36 – 8.3 Galatians 2.15–21 **Passage for Memorization/Meditation:** Galatians 2.20

KINGDOMTIDE: PROPER 7
The Headship, Harvest, and Hope of Christ

Color: Green
Renewal, New Life

Prayer: O Lord, make us have constant love and reverence for your holy Name, for you never fail to help and lead those whom you have set upon the sure foundation of your loving kindness; through Jesus Christ our Lord, who lives and reigns with you and the Holy Spirit, one God, forever and ever. Amen.

YEAR A	**Lectionary Topic:** *Proclaim Christ Boldly* **Texts:** Genesis 21.8–21 Psalm 86.1–10, 16–17 Matthew 10.24–39 Romans 6.1–11 **Passage for Memorization/Meditation:** Romans 6.3–4
YEAR B	**Lectionary Topic:** *Peace, Be Still* **Texts:** 1 Samuel 17.1–51 Psalm 9.9–20 Mark 4.35–41 2 Corinthians 6.1–13 **Passage for Memorization/Meditation:** 1 Samuel 17.47
YEAR C	**Lectionary Topic:** *Jesus Terrifies the Demons* **Texts:** 1 Kings 19.1–15 Psalm 42 and 43 Luke 8.26–39 Galatians 3.23–29 **Passage for Memorization/Meditation:** Galatians 3.27–28

KINGDOMTIDE: PROPER 8
The Headship, Harvest, and Hope of Christ

Color: Green
Renewal, New Life

Prayer: Almighty God, you have built your Church upon the foundation of the apostles and prophets, Jesus Christ himself being the chief cornerstone: Grant us so to be joined together in unity of spirit by their teaching, that we may be made a holy temple acceptable to you; through Jesus Christ our Lord, who lives and reigns with you and the Holy Spirit, one God, forever and ever. Amen.

YEAR A	**Lectionary Topic:** *The Reward of Righteousness* **Texts:** Genesis 22.1–19 Psalm 13 Matthew 10.40–42 Romans 6.12–23 **Passage for Memorization/Meditation:** Romans 6.12–13
YEAR B	**Lectionary Topic:** *Your Faith Has Made You Well* **Texts:** 2 Samuel 1.1, 17–27 Psalm 130 Mark 5.21–43 2 Corinthians 8.7–15 **Passage for Memorization/Meditation:** 2 Corinthians 8.9
YEAR C	**Lectionary Topic:** *The Cost of Following Jesus* **Texts:** 2 Kings 2.1–2, 6–14 Psalm 77.1–2, 11–20 Luke 9.51–62 Galatians 5.1, 13–25 **Passage for Memorization/Meditation:** Galatians 5.22–23

KINGDOMTIDE: PROPER 9
The Headship, Harvest, and Hope of Christ

Color: Green
Renewal, New Life

Prayer: O God, you have taught us to keep all your commandments by loving you and our neighbor: Grant us the grace of your Holy Spirit, that we may be devoted to you with our whole heart, and united to one another with pure affection; through Jesus Christ our Lord, who lives and reigns with you and the Holy Spirit, one God, forever and ever. Amen.

YEAR A	**Lectionary Topic:** *His Easy Yoke and Light Burden* **Texts:** Genesis 24.34–67 Psalm 45.10–17 Matthew 11.16–30 Romans 7.15–25 **Passage for Memorization/Meditation:** Matthew 11.28–30
YEAR B	**Lectionary Topic:** *Authorized and Sent by Christ* **Texts:** 2 Samuel 5.1–10 Psalm 48 Mark 6.1–13 2 Corinthians 12.2–10 **Passage for Memorization/Meditation:** 2 Corinthians 12.9–10
YEAR C	**Lectionary Topic:** *Authority Over the Power of Satan* **Texts:** 2 Kings 5.1–14 Psalm 30 Luke 10.1–20 Galatians 6.1–16 **Passage for Memorization/Meditation:** Luke 10.18–20

KINGDOMTIDE: PROPER 10
The Headship, Harvest, and Hope of Christ

Color: Green
Renewal, New Life

Prayer: O Lord, mercifully receive the prayers of your people who call upon you, and grant that we may know and understand your will, and also may have grace and power faithfully to carry it out; through Jesus Christ our Lord, who lives and reigns with you and the Holy Spirit, one God, now and forever. Amen.

YEAR A	**Lectionary Topic:** *The Fruitful Word of the Kingdom* **Texts:** Genesis 25.19–34 Psalm 119.105–112 Matthew 13.1–23 Romans 8.1–11 **Passage for Memorization/Meditation:** Romans 8.1
YEAR B	**Lectionary Topic:** *The Death of John the Baptist* **Texts:** 2 Samuel 6.1–5, 12b–19 Psalm 24 Mark 6.14–29 Ephesians 1.3–14 **Passage for Memorization/Meditation:** Ephesians 1.3–4
YEAR C	**Lectionary Topic:** *Who Is My Neighbor?* **Texts:** Amos 7.7–17 Psalm 82 Luke 10.25–37 Colossians 1.1–14 **Passage for Memorization/Meditation:** Colossians 1.13–14

KINGDOMTIDE: PROPER 11
The Headship, Harvest, and Hope of Christ

Color: Green
Renewal, New Life

Prayer: Almighty God, the fountain of all wisdom, you know our needs before we ask and our complete dependence upon you: Have compassion on our weakness, and mercifully give us those things which we are unworthy or too blind to request for ourselves; through the worthiness of your Son Jesus Christ our Lord, who lives and reigns with you and the Holy Spirit, one God, now and forever. Amen.

YEAR **A**	**Lectionary Topic:** *The Harvest at the End of the Age* **Texts:** Genesis 28.10–19 Psalm 139.1–12, 23–24 Matthew 13.24–43 Romans 8.12–25 **Passage for Memorization/Meditation:** Romans 8.20–21
YEAR **B**	**Lectionary Topic:** *Sheep Without a Shepherd* **Texts:** 2 Samuel 7.1–14 Psalm 89.20–37 Mark 6.30–34, 53–56 Ephesians 2.11–22 **Passage for Memorization/Meditation:** 2 Samuel 7.13–14
YEAR **C**	**Lectionary Topic:** *Sit at the Lord's Feet* **Texts:** Amos 8.1–12 Psalm 52 Luke 10.38–42 Colossians 1.15–28 **Passage for Memorization/Meditation:** Colossians 1.15–16

KINGDOMTIDE: PROPER 12
The Headship, Harvest, and Hope of Christ

Color: Green
Renewal, New Life

Prayer: O God, the protector of all who trust in you, without whom nothing is strong, nothing is holy: Increase and multiply upon us your mercy; that, with you as our ruler and guide, we may live in this life to gain an eternal reward; through Jesus Christ our Lord, who lives and reigns with you and the Holy Spirit, one God, forever and ever. Amen.

YEAR **A**	**Lectionary Topic:** *The Hidden Treasure* **Texts:** Genesis 29.15–28 Psalm 105.1–11, 45b Matthew 13.44–52 Romans 8.26–39 **Passage for Memorization/Meditation:** Romans 8.37–39
YEAR **B**	**Lectionary Topic:** *Jesus Feeds the Hungry* **Texts:** 2 Samuel 11.1–15 Psalm 14 John 6.1–21 Ephesians 3.14–21 **Passage for Memorization/Meditation:** Ephesians 3.20–21
YEAR **C**	**Lectionary Topic:** *Lord, Teach Us To Pray* **Texts:** Hosea 1.2–10 Psalm 85 Luke 11.1–13 Colossians 2.6–19 **Passage for Memorization/Meditation:** Colossians 2.15

KINGDOMTIDE: PROPER 13
The Headship, Harvest, and Hope of Christ

Color: Green
Renewal, New Life

Prayer: Let your continual mercy, O Lord, cleanse and defend your Church; and, because it cannot continue in safety without your help, protect and govern it always by your goodness; through Jesus Christ our Lord, who lives and reigns with you and the Holy Spirit, one God, forever and ever. Amen.

YEAR **A**	**Lectionary Topic:** *Jesus Feeds the Hungry* **Texts:** Genesis 32.22–31 Psalm 17.1–7, 15 Matthew 14.13–21 Romans 9.1–5 **Passage for Memorization/Meditation:** Matthew 14.19–20
YEAR **B**	**Lectionary Topic:** *The Bread of Life* **Texts:** 2 Samuel 11.26 – 12.13 Psalm 51.1–12 John 6.24–35 Ephesians 4.1–16 **Passage for Memorization/Meditation:** Ephesians 4.4–6
YEAR **C**	**Lectionary Topic:** *Be Rich Toward God* **Texts:** Hosea 11.1–11 Psalm 107.1–9, 43 Luke 12.13–21 Colossians 3.1–11 **Passage for Memorization/Meditation:** Colossians 3.1–2

KINGDOMTIDE: PROPER 14
The Headship, Harvest, and Hope of Christ

Color: Green
Renewal, New Life

Prayer: Grant to us, Lord, we pray, the spirit to think and do always those things that are right, that we, who cannot exist without you, may be enabled to stand firm against all the schemes of the enemy; through Jesus Christ our Lord, who lives and reigns with you and the Holy Spirit, one God, forever and ever. Amen.

YEAR **A**	**Lectionary Topic:** *Do Not Be Afraid* **Texts:** Genesis 37.1–28 Psalm 105.1–6, 16–22, 45b Matthew 14.22–33 Romans 10.5–15 **Passage for Memorization/Meditation:** Romans 10.9–10
YEAR **B**	**Lectionary Topic:** *The Body of Christ, the Bread of Heaven* **Texts:** 2 Samuel 18.5–33 Psalm 130 John 6.35–51 Ephesians 4.25 — 5.2 **Passage for Memorization/Meditation:** John 6.51
YEAR **C**	**Lectionary Topic:** *You Must Be Ready* **Texts:** Isaiah 1.1, 10–20 Psalm 50.1–8, 22–23 Luke 12.32–40 Hebrews 11.1–16 **Passage for Memorization/Meditation:** Hebrews 11.1

KINGDOMTIDE: PROPER 15
The Headship, Harvest, and Hope of Christ

Color: Green
Renewal, New Life

Prayer: Almighty God, you have given your only Son to be for us a sacrifice for sin, and also an example of godly life: Give us grace to receive thankfully the fruits of his redeeming work, and to follow daily in the blessed steps of his most holy life; through Jesus Christ your Son our Lord, who lives and reigns with you and the Holy Spirit, one God, now and forever. Amen.

YEAR **A**	**Lectionary Topic:** *Cleanse Your Heart* **Texts:** Genesis 45.1–15 Psalm 133 Matthew 15.10–28 Romans 11.1–2, 29–32 **Passage for Memorization/Meditation:** Romans 11.29
YEAR **B**	**Lectionary Topic:** *The Blood of Christ, the Cup of Salvation* **Texts:** 1 Kings 3.3–14 Psalm 111 John 6.51–58 Ephesians 5.15–20 **Passage for Memorization/Meditation:** John 6.53–54
YEAR **C**	**Lectionary Topic:** *Christ Brings Fire and Divisions* **Texts:** Isaiah 5.1–7 Psalm 80.1–2, 8–19 Luke 12.49–56 Hebrews 11.29 — 12.2 **Passage for Memorization/Meditation:** Hebrews 12.1–2

KINGDOMTIDE: PROPER 16
The Headship, Harvest, and Hope of Christ

Color: Green
Renewal, New Life

Prayer: Grant, O merciful God, that your Church, being gathered together in unity by your Holy Spirit, may show forth your power among all peoples, to the glory of your Name; through Jesus Christ our Lord, who lives and reigns with you and the Holy Spirit, one God, forever and ever. Amen.

YEAR **A**	**Lectionary Topic:** *Christ, the Son of the Living God* **Texts:** Exodus 1.8—2.10 Psalm 124 Matthew 16.13–20 Romans 12.1–8 **Passage for Memorization/Meditation:** Matthew 16.15–16
YEAR **B**	**Lectionary Topic:** *Our Spiritual Battle* **Texts:** 1 Kings 8.1–11, 22–52 Psalm 84 John 6.56–69 Ephesians 6.10–20 **Passage for Memorization/Meditation:** Ephesians 6.11–12
YEAR **C**	**Lectionary Topic:** *Set Free from Satan's Bondage* **Texts:** Isaiah 58.9–14 Psalm 103.1–8 Luke 13.10–17 Hebrews 12.18–29 **Passage for Memorization/Meditation:** Hebrews 12.28–29

KINGDOMTIDE: PROPER 17
The Headship, Harvest, and Hope of Christ

Color: Green
Renewal, New Life

Prayer: Lord of all power and might, the author and giver of all good things: Implant in our hearts the love of your Name; increase in us true devotion; nourish us with spiritual food; and bring forth in us the fruit of kingdom works; through Jesus Christ our Lord, who lives and reigns with you and the Holy Spirit, one God forever and ever. Amen.

YEAR **A**	**Lectionary Topic:** *Take Up Your Cross* **Texts:** Exodus 3.1–15 Psalm 105.1–6, 23–26, 45b Matthew 16.21–28 Romans 12.9–21 **Passage for Memorization/Meditation:** Romans 12.9
YEAR **B**	**Lectionary Topic:** *A Heart to Obey God* **Texts:** Song of Solomon 2.8–13 Psalm 45.1–2, 6–9 Mark 7.1–23 James 1.17–27 **Passage for Memorization/Meditation:** James 1.22
YEAR **C**	**Lectionary Topic:** *The Humble Will Be Exalted* **Texts:** Jeremiah 2.4–13 Psalm 81.1, 10–16 Luke 14.1, 7–14 Hebrews 13.1–8 **Passage for Memorization/Meditation:** Hebrews 13.7–8

KINGDOMTIDE: PROPER 18
The Headship, Harvest, and Hope of Christ

Color: Green
Renewal, New Life

Prayer: Grant us, O Lord, to trust in you with all our hearts; for you always resist the proud who confide in their own strength, but you never forsake those who make their boast of your mercy; through Jesus Christ our Lord, who lives and reigns with you and the Holy Spirit, one God, now and forever. Amen.

YEAR A	**Lectionary Topic:** *Dealing with Sin in the Church* **Texts:** Exodus 12.1–14 Psalm 149 Matthew 18.15–20 Romans 13.8–14 **Passage for Memorization/Meditation:** Matthew 18.15–17
YEAR B	**Lectionary Topic:** *Christ Has Done All Things Well* **Texts:** Proverbs 22.2, 8–9, 22–23 Psalm 125 Mark 7.24–36 James 2.1–17 **Passage for Memorization/Meditation:** James 2.5
YEAR C	**Lectionary Topic:** *Count the Cost* **Texts:** Jeremiah 18.1–11 Psalm 139.1–6, 13–18 Luke 14.25–33 Philemon 1–21 **Passage for Memorization/Meditation:** Luke 14.27–28

KINGDOMTIDE: PROPER 19
The Headship, Harvest, and Hope of Christ

Color: *Green*
Renewal, New Life

Prayer: O God, without you we are not able to honor you; mercifully grant that your Holy Spirit may in all things direct and rule our hearts; through Jesus Christ our Lord, who lives and reigns with you and the Holy Spirit, one God, now and forever. Amen.

YEAR A	**Lectionary Topic:** *God's Forgiveness* **Texts:** Exodus 14.19–31 *Exodus 15:1b–11, 20–21 (Psalm for the Week)* Matthew 18.21–35 Romans 14.1–12 **Passage for Memorization/Meditation:** Exodus 15.2–3
YEAR B	**Lectionary Topic:** *Self Death* **Texts:** Proverbs 1.20–33 Psalm 19 Mark 8.27–38 James 3.1–12 **Passage for Memorization/Meditation:** Mark 8.35–36
YEAR C	**Lectionary Topic:** *Heaven Rejoices When Sinners Repent* **Texts:** Jeremiah 4.11–12, 22–28 Psalm 14 Luke 15.1–10 1 Timothy 1.12–17 **Passage for Memorization/Meditation:** 1 Timothy 1.15–16

KINGDOMTIDE: PROPER 20
The Headship, Harvest, and Hope of Christ

Color: Green
Renewal, New Life

Prayer: Grant us, Lord, not to be anxious about earthly things, but to love things heavenly; and even now, while we are placed among things that are passing away, to hold fast to those that shall endure; through Jesus Christ our Lord, who lives and reigns with you and the Holy Spirit, one God, forever and ever. Amen.

YEAR A	**Lectionary Topic:** *The Last Will Be First*
	Texts: Exodus 16.2–15 Psalm 105.1–6, 37–45 Matthew 20.1–16 Philippians 1.21–30
	Passage for Memorization/Meditation: Philippians 1.21
YEAR B	**Lectionary Topic:** *Be a Servant of All*
	Texts: Proverbs 31.10–31 Psalm 1 Mark 9.30–37 James 3.13 — 4.8
	Passage for Memorization/Meditation: James 4.7–8
YEAR C	**Lectionary Topic:** *You Cannot Serve God and Money*
	Texts: Jeremiah 8.18 — 9.1 Psalm 79.1–9 Luke 16.1–13 1 Timothy 2.1–7
	Passage for Memorization/Meditation: Luke 16.13

KINGDOMTIDE: PROPER 21
The Headship, Harvest, and Hope of Christ

Color: Green
Renewal, New Life

Prayer: O God, you declare your almighty power by showing mercy and pity: Grant us the fullness of your grace, that we, running to obtain your promises, may receive an imperishable prize; through Jesus Christ our Lord, who lives and reigns with you and the Holy Spirit, one God, forever and ever. Amen.

YEAR A	**Lectionary Topic:** *God's People Resisting His Will* **Texts:** Exodus 17.1–7 Psalm 78.1–4, 12–16 Matthew 21.23–32 Philippians 2.1–13 **Passage for Memorization/Meditation:** Philippians 2.12–13
YEAR B	**Lectionary Topic:** *Wage War Against Sin* **Texts:** Esther 7.1–10 Psalm 124 Mark 9.38–50 James 5.13–20 **Passage for Memorization/Meditation:** James 5.15–16
YEAR C	**Lectionary Topic:** *Reject Greed and Care for the Poor* **Texts:** Jeremiah 32.1, 2, 6–15 Psalm 91.1–6, 14–16 Luke 16.19–31 1 Timothy 6.6–19 **Passage for Memorization/Meditation:** 1 Timothy 6.10

KINGDOMTIDE: PROPER 22
The Headship, Harvest, and Hope of Christ

Color: Green
Renewal, New Life

Prayer: Almighty and everlasting God, you are always more ready to hear than we to pray, and to give more than we deserve: Pour upon us the abundance of your mercy, forgiving us of offenses that we are too ignorant to confess, and giving us those good things for which we are not worthy to ask, except through Jesus Christ our Savior; who lives and reigns with you and the Holy Spirit, one God, for ever and ever. Amen.

YEAR A	**Lectionary Topic:** *Christ Our Cornerstone* **Texts:** Exodus 20.1–20 Psalm 19 Matthew 21.33–46 Philippians 3.4–14 **Passage for Memorization/Meditation:** Philippians 3.13–14
YEAR B	**Lectionary Topic:** *Joined Together By God* **Texts:** Job 2.1–10 Psalm 26 Mark 10.2–16 Hebrews 1.1–4; 2.5–12 **Passage for Memorization/Meditation:** Hebrews 1.3
YEAR C	**Lectionary Topic:** *Increase Our Faith* **Texts:** Lamentations 1.1–6 Psalm 137 Luke 17.5–10 2 Timothy 1.1–14 **Passage for Memorization/Meditation:** Luke 17.5–6

KINGDOMTIDE: PROPER 23
The Headship, Harvest, and Hope of Christ

Color: Green
Renewal, New Life

Prayer: Lord, we pray that your grace may always precede and follow us; and that we would be valiant warriors because it is you who treads down our foe, through Jesus Christ our Lord, who lives and reigns with you and the Holy Spirit, one God, now and forever. Amen.

YEAR A	**Lectionary Topic:** *Many Are Called, but Few Are Chosen* **Texts:** Exodus 32.1–14 Psalm 106.1–6, 19–23 Matthew 22.1–14 Philippians 4.1–9 **Passage for Memorization/Meditation:** Philippians 4.8
YEAR B	**Lectionary Topic:** *Leave Everything and Follow Him* **Texts:** Job 23.1–17 Psalm 22.1–15 Mark 10.17–31 Hebrews 4.12–16 **Passage for Memorization/Meditation:** Hebrews 4.15
YEAR C	**Lectionary Topic:** *Give Praise to God* **Texts:** Jeremiah 29.1, 4–14 Psalm 66.1–12 Luke 17.11–19 2 Timothy 2.8–15 **Passage for Memorization/Meditation:** 2 Timothy 2.15

KINGDOMTIDE: PROPER 24
The Headship, Harvest, and Hope of Christ

Color: Green
Renewal, New Life

Prayer: Almighty and everlasting God, in Christ you have revealed your glory among the nations: Outfit us with your full armor, that your Church throughout the world may persevere with steadfast faith in the confession of your Name; through Jesus Christ our Lord, who lives and reigns with you and the Holy Spirit, one God, forever and ever. Amen.

YEAR **A**	**Lectionary Topic:** *Give to God What Is His* **Texts:** Exodus 33.12–23 Psalm 99 Matthew 22.15–22 1 Thessalonians 1.1–10 **Passage for Memorization/Meditation:** 1 Thessalonians 1.9–10
YEAR **B**	**Lectionary Topic:** *Christ Our Ransom* **Texts:** Job 38.1–7 Psalm 104.1–9, 24, 35b Mark 10.35–45 Hebrews 5.1–10 **Passage for Memorization/Meditation:** Mark 10.45
YEAR **C**	**Lectionary Topic:** *Cry Out To God* **Texts:** Jeremiah 31.27–34 Psalm 119.97–104 Luke 18.1–8 2 Timothy 3.14 — 4.5 **Passage for Memorization/Meditation:** 2 Timothy 3.16–17

KINGDOMTIDE: PROPER 25

The Headship, Harvest, and Hope of Christ

Color: Green
Renewal, New Life

Prayer: Almighty and everlasting God, increase in us the gifts of faith, hope, and love; and, so that we represent you faithfully, make us love what you command; through Jesus Christ our Lord, who lives and reigns with you and the Holy Spirit, one God, forever and ever. Amen.

YEAR A	**Lectionary Topic:** *The Great Commandment* **Texts:** Deuteronomy 34.1–12 Psalm 90.1–6, 13–17 Matthew 22.34–46 1 Thessalonians 2.1–8 **Passage for Memorization/Meditation:** Matthew 22.37–39
YEAR B	**Lectionary Topic:** *Jesus, Have Mercy On Me* **Texts:** Job 42.1–6, 10–17 Psalm 34.1–8 [19–22] Mark 10.46–52 Hebrews 7.23–28 **Passage for Memorization/Meditation:** Hebrews 7.25
YEAR C	**Lectionary Topic:** *God, Be Merciful to Me, a Sinner* **Texts:** Joel 2.23–32 Psalm 65 Luke 18.9–14 2 Timothy 4.6–8, 16–18 **Passage for Memorization/Meditation:** Luke 18.13

ALL SAINTS DAY OBSERVED
The Communion of Saints

Color: Red
Blood of Martyrs

Prayer: Almighty God, you have knit together your elect in one communion and fellowship in the body of your Son Christ our Lord: Give us the grace to follow your blessed saints in all virtuous and godly living, that we may stand unashamed among those who truly love you; through Jesus Christ our Lord, who with you and the Holy Spirit lives and reigns, one God, in glory everlasting. Amen.

YEAR **A**	**Lectionary Topic:** *The Communion of Saints* **Texts:** Revelation 7.9–17 Psalm 34 Matthew 5.1–12 1 John 3.1–3 **Passage for Memorization/Meditation:** 1 John 3.2–3
YEAR **B**	**Lectionary Topic:** *The Communion of Saints* **Texts:** Isaiah 25.6–9 Psalm 24 John 11.32–44 Revelation 21.1–6 **Passage for Memorization/Meditation:** Revelation 21.3–4
YEAR **C**	**Lectionary Topic:** *The Communion of Saints* **Texts:** Daniel 7.1–3, 15–18 Psalm 149 Luke 6.20–31 Ephesians 1.11–23 **Passage for Memorization/Meditation:** Ephesians 1.22–23

KINGDOMTIDE: PROPER 27
The Headship, Harvest, and Hope of Christ

Color: Green
Renewal, New Life

Prayer: O God, whose blessed Son came into the world that he might destroy the works of the devil and make us children of God and heirs of eternal life: Grant that, having this hope, we may purify ourselves as he is pure; that, when he comes again with power and great glory, we may be made like him in his eternal and glorious kingdom; where he lives and reigns with you and the Holy Spirit, one God, forever and ever. Amen.

YEAR **A**	**Lectionary Topic:** *Be Ready for the Bridegroom* **Texts:** Joshua 24.1–25 Psalm 78.1–7 Matthew 25.1–13 1 Thessalonians 4.13–18 **Passage for Memorization/Meditation:** 1 Thessalonians 4.16–17
YEAR **B**	**Lectionary Topic:** *The Offering God Desires* **Texts:** Ruth 3.1–5; 4.13–17 Psalm 127 Mark 12.38–44 Hebrews 9.24–28 **Passage for Memorization/Meditation:** Hebrews 9.27–28
YEAR **C**	**Lectionary Topic:** *God Raises the Dead to Life* **Texts:** Haggai 2.1–9 Psalm 145.1–5, 17–21 Luke 20.27–38 2 Thessalonians 2.1–17 **Passage for Memorization/Meditation:** 2 Thessalonians 2.14–15

KINGDOMTIDE: PROPER 28
The Headship, Harvest, and Hope of Christ

Color: Green
Renewal, New Life

Prayer: Blessed Lord, who caused all holy Scriptures to be written for our instruction: Grant us so to hear them, read, learn, and inwardly digest them, that we may embrace and ever hold fast the blessed hope of eternal life, which you have given us in our Savior Jesus Christ; who lives and reigns with you and the Holy Spirit, one God, forever and ever. Amen.

YEAR **A**	**Lectionary Topic:** *Well Done, Good and Faithful Servant* **Texts:** Judges 4.1–7 Psalm 123 Matthew 25.14–30 1 Thessalonians 5.1–11 **Passage for Memorization/Meditation:** Matthew 25.21
YEAR **B**	**Lectionary Topic:** *The End Is Coming* **Texts:** 1 Samuel 1.4–20 *1 Samuel 2.1–10 (Psalm of the Week)* Mark 13.1–8 Hebrews 10.11–25 **Passage for Memorization/Meditation:** Hebrews 10.23–25
YEAR **C**	**Lectionary Topic:** *Endure Until the King Appears* **Texts:** Isaiah 65.17–25 Psalm 98 Luke 21.5–19 2 Thessalonians 3.6–13 **Passage for Memorization/Meditation:** Isaiah 65.25

THE REIGN OF CHRIST THE KING

The King of Kings

Color: Gold

Light, Presence of God

Prayer: Almighty and everlasting God, whose will it is to restore all things in your well beloved Son, the King of kings and Lord of lords: Mercifully grant that the peoples of the earth, divided and enslaved by sin, may be freed from Satan and brought together under Christ's gracious rule; who lives and reigns with you and the Holy Spirit, one God, now and forever. Amen.

YEAR **A**	**Lectionary Topic:** *The King of Kings* **Texts:** Ezekiel 34.11–24 Psalm 100 Matthew 25.31–46 Ephesians 1.15–23 **Passage for Memorization/Meditation:** Matthew 25.40
YEAR **B**	**Lectionary Topic:** *The King of Kings* **Texts:** 2 Samuel 23.1–7 Psalm 132.1–12 [13–18] John 18.33–37 Revelation 1.4–8 **Passage for Memorization/Meditation:** John 18.36
YEAR **C**	**Lectionary Topic:** *The King of Kings* **Texts:** Jeremiah 23.1–6 Psalm 46 Luke 23.33–43 Colossians 1.11–20 **Passage for Memorization/Meditation:** Colossians 1.18

5

APPENDICES

Appendix 1

THE CTV LOGO

 The CTV logo is a combination of two symbols historically related to the theme of *Christus Victor*.

The Victor's Cross

This ancient cross reads 'Jesus Christ, Victor' (in Greek, Ιησους Χριστος, Νικα). The first two words are abbreviated to the first and last letters (indicated by the lines over the letters). While the specific origin of this symbol is unknown, it is clear that this cross was an important symbol to the church, even appearing on the back of ancient coins. The CTV logo is specifically patterned after the Victor's Cross. The shape of the square cross with lettering in the quadrants is obvious in our logo. The use of this cross as a coin gives rise to our use of it in a round form. The Greek words are replaced by initials with the square cross itself being used as a form of T to complete CTV. CTV intentionally seeks to embody the ancient faith for new generations of urban Christians. We join with the ancient church in using this cross to symbolize the victory of the kingdom of God through Jesus Christ.

The Regnant Lamb

The Regnant Lamb (or lamb who reigns as king) is another important ancient symbol of the theme of *Christus Victor*. This symbol brings together the two movements of the work of Christ: his *humble descent* from heaven to earth to the grave (humiliation) and his *victorious ascent* from the grave to resurrection life to the right hand of the Father (exaltation). The victory of Christ was won not with military might but with the humble suffering of the Lamb of God. This symbol shows the Lamb of God raised in victory (shown through his halo) and exalted as Lord and King (shown through the royal scepter in the shape of the cross). [23] Our logo seeks to

represent this symbol by use of the crown of thorns; another symbol that brings together the humiliation and exaltation of Christ. The thorns clearly display his suffering and death as the Lamb of God. Yet they are a crown, pointing us to the victory and reign of our Lord and King. Our adoption of the *Christus Victor* theme is not a claim of triumph that exempts us from difficulty or suffering. CTV uses this ancient symbol to affirm that the path of victory is the path of the cross. "We suffer with him in order that we may also be glorified with him" (Rom 8.17, ESV).

---

[23] Sacred Roots images – © 2009. The Urban Ministry Institute. All Rights Reserved. For more information on Sacred Roots, please visit www.tumi.org.

Appendix 2

THE NICENE CREED WITH BIBLICAL SUPPORT AND EXPLANATION

(Adapted from *The Nicene Creed with Biblical Support for Each Section,* TUMI)

We believe in one God, (Deuteronomy 6.4–5, Mark 12.29, 1 Corinthians 8.6)

> *The One God is the Trinity. He is one being who exists eternally in three persons, the Father, the Son, and the Spirit.*

the Father Almighty, (Genesis 17.1, Daniel 4.35, Matthew 6.9, Ephesians 4.6, Revelation 1.8)

> *The Lord is all powerful. His might and ability have no limit. This Almighty God is a tender, loving Father for his people.*

the maker of heaven and earth, (Genesis 1.1, Isaiah 40.28, Revelation 10.6)

> *The Lord is the true originator of everything in our universe. He created all that exists from nothing.*

of everything that exists, whether visible or invisible. (Psalm 148, Romans 11.36, Revelation 4.11)

> *Indeed, every being and object in existence was created by the Lord. Even spiritual entities such as Satan and his demons are the Lord's creation. As creator, the Lord is due the worship and obedience of everything he has created.*

We believe in one Lord, Jesus Christ, the one and only Son of God, who was begotten of the Father before time. He is God as the Father is God, Light as the Father is Light, truly God as the Father is truly

God, begotten, but not a created being. He and the Father are of the same substance. (John 1.1–2, 3.16–18, 8.58, 14.9–10, 20.28, Colossians 1.15–17, Hebrews 1.3–6)

> *God the Son, who on earth was called Jesus, is equal with the Father. He is neither created nor subordinated. In all ways, he shares the nature of the Father and the Spirit.*

Everything was created through him. (John 1.3, Colossians 1.16)

> *God created by the power of his word. Jesus himself is called the Word, or the revelation of God. It was through the agency of the Son that God created.*

Who for us and for our salvation came down from heaven and took on flesh through the Holy Spirit and the Virgin Mary, and thus became fully human. (Matthew 1.20–23, John 1.14, 6.38, Luke 19.10)

> *In the fullness of time, God the Son was born as a human baby. He took on a fully human nature without sacrificing any aspect of his divine nature, uniting them in one person. The two natures exist in one person without confusion, without change, without division, without separation.*

For our sake, he was crucified under Pontius Pilate, he suffered death and was buried, (Matthew 27.1–2, Mark 15.24–39, 15.43–47, Acts 13.29, Romans 5.8, 1 Corinthians 15.3–4, Hebrews 2.10, 13.12)

> *Jesus, God the Son, truly and bodily suffered, died, and was buried. He died as the atoning sacrifice for sin, and not only for our sin, but for the sin of the whole world.*

and he rose again on the third day according to the Scriptures. (Mark 16.5–7, Luke 24.6–8, Acts 1.3, Romans 6.9, 10.9, 1 Corinthians 15.4–6, 2 Timothy 2.8)

> *Jesus was truly and bodily raised from the dead on the third day. He appeared to the disciples and to many believers, proving himself to be alive with many signs. His resurrection proved his victory over sin, death, and Satan.*

He went up into heaven where he is seated at the right hand of the Father. (Luke 24.50–53, Acts 1.9–11, 7.55–56, Ephesians 1.19–20)

> *Jesus ascended into heaven, and was exalted to the right hand of the Father where he took his seat because his saving work was complete.*

He will come again in glory to judge the living and the dead. His kingdom will never end. (Isaiah 9.7, Matthew 24.30, John 5.22, Acts 1.11, 17.31, Romans 14.9, 2 Corinthians 5.10, 2 Timothy 4.1)

> *One day very soon, Jesus will return to gather his bride, the redeemed of all ages, and make complete the victory initially won at the cross.*

We believe in the Holy Spirit, the Lord, and life-giver. (Genesis 1.1–2, Job 33.4, Psalm 104.30, 139.7–8, Luke 4.18–19, John 3.5–6, Acts 1.1–2, 1 Corinthians 2.11, Revelation 3.22)

> *The Holy Spirit is an equal member of the Trinity with the Father and the Son. He is the agent through whom we experience the presence of God, new life, and Christ's lordship.*

He comes from the Father and the Son. (John 14.16–18, 14.26, 15.26, 20.22)

> *The Spirit was sent by the Father and the Son upon the return of the Son to heaven.*

He is to be worshipped and glorified with the Father and the Son. (Isaiah 6.3, Matthew 28.19, 2 Corinthians 13.14, Revelation 4.8)

As an equal member of the Trinity, the Spirit is equally deserving of our worship, our attention, and our obedience. We should neither underemphasize the Spirit, nor emphasize the Spirit over the Father and the Son.

He spoke through the prophets. (Numbers 11.29, Micah 3.8, Acts 2.17–18, 2 Peter 1.21)

The 66 books of the Bible are God-breathed. They are inspired by God, through the work of the Spirit. They are without error, and form an infallible guide to life and faith. Each and every word of the Bible is inspired. Inspiration does not overrule the style, personalities, or purposes of the human authors, but works with them to speak the exact word of the Lord.

We believe in one holy worldwide apostolic church. (Matthew 16.18, Ephesians 4.4–6, 5.25–28, 1 Corinthians 1.2, 10.17, 1 Timothy 3.15, Revelation 7.9)

The church is the bride and body of Christ. It is the arena and agent of God's kingdom on earth today, and is central to all that God is doing in the world. The identity, mission, and doctrine of the church are set by the biblical apostles of Jesus. The universal church is made up of believers from all times and in all places. Local expressions of the universal church should have the Word rightly preached, the sacraments rightly administered, and discipline rightly practiced. The church is absolutely essential in the life of the believer.

We acknowledge one baptism for the forgiveness of sin. (Acts 2.38–39, 22.16, 1 Peter 3.21, Ephesians 4.4–5)

> *Salvation is given from God by grace alone, through faith alone in Christ alone, not by works. At initial salvation, the believer receives the baptism of the Spirit, where the fullness of the Holy Spirit comes to dwell in the Christian. Water baptism is a public sign that a person has repented of sins, received forgiveness of sins, died with Christ to sin, been raised to newness of life and received the Holy Spirit. Baptism is a sign of the believer's incorporation into the body of Christ as expressed in the local church. Baptism is also a pledge to serve Christ according to the gifts given to each person.*

We anticipate the resurrection of the dead and the life of the age to come. (Isaiah 11.6–10, Micah 4.1–7, Luke 18.29–30, Revelation 21.1–5, 21.22–22.5)

> *One day, at the return of Christ, all the redeemed of earth who have died will be resurrected to eternal life, just as Christ was. Those who are alive at his coming will be changed from mortality to immortality. Our eternal dwelling will be with God in a new heavens and a new earth, free from the death, pain, sin, and curse of our present world. We will live with him in eternal bliss and perfect communion.*

Amen.

Appendix 3

THE TERM 'CATHOLIC'

The History and Meaning of 'Catholic'

CTV retains the use of the word 'catholic' in our affirmation of the
Nicene Creed. We understand that for many this term presents some
difficulty. However, we believe it to be an important term both
historically and presently. When understood accurately, 'catholic' is
a vital and precious term for the church.

In the time of the ancient church, the Greek word *katholikē*
(καθολική) had a common usage meaning 'general, universal.'[24]
Ignatius of Antioch (AD 35–108) was the first to use the term with
specific reference to the church. He writes in his *Letter to the
Smyrneans*, §8.2, "*Wherever the bishop appears, there let the congregation
be; just as wherever Jesus Christ is, there is **the catholic church**.*"[25]

Ignatius and the early fathers used the term in its generic sense of
'universal' to refer to the whole scope of the body of Christ. By the
time of the Council of Nicaea (AD 325) it had developed a special
secondary connotation with reference to the church. The catholic
church not only referred to the one church in Jesus Christ united
across space and time but also distinguished orthodox apostolic
church from the wide variety of heretical splinter movements.

During the Roman era of the church (500–1500) 'Catholic' came to
refer specifically to the visible structure of the Western Roman
Church (first, as opposed to the Eastern Orthodox Church, then later
as opposed to the Protestant Churches and the Church of England).

---

[24] Arndt, William, Frederick W. Danker, and Walter Bauer. *A Greek-English Lexicon of
the New Testament and Other Early Christian Literature* (Chicago: University of Chicago
Press, 2000), 493.
[25] *The Apostolic Fathers: Greek Texts and English Translations*, 3rd Ed. Michael Holmes,
ed. and trans (Baker Academic, 2007), 255, *emphasis* added.

The term itself, however, is not uniquely tied to any branch of the church, but rather refers to the entire body of genuine Christians no matter the place, time, or expression.

Objections and Suggested Alternatives

Because of a false identification of the term 'catholic' with the Roman Catholic Church, Protestant Christians have very often objected to the word and sought substitutes.

One common objection is "The word 'catholic' is not in the Bible!" This is absolutely true. The Greek term *katholikē* appears in neither the New Testament, nor in the Septuagint (the Greek translation of the Old Testament). This, however, does not automatically disqualify it from being an important or even an essential Christian term.

There are certain terms that the church has either invented or chosen to describe or summarize the teaching of Scripture. Through long and rich histories of usage, these terms have become extremely important for the church. Some examples of this kind of term are Trinity (used to describe the way in which God is one and God is three), God-man (used to describe the way in which Christ is fully God and fully human), incarnation (used to summarize the story of the Son taking on flesh), and inerrant (used to describe the truthfulness of Scripture). It is into this category that the term catholic clearly falls. While catholic is not used in Scripture, its rich history of usage in the church has rendered it extremely important.

A common way to grapple with the difficulty of the term is to distinguish between big 'C' Catholic and little 'c' catholic. This distinction reflects the difference between the name of a particular branch of the church, Catholic, and the adjective used by the ancient church, catholic. In some ways this is helpful. It does clarify that the word itself does not refer only to the Roman Catholic Church. However, it does not explain everything. The main problem is that it is a false distinction. Applying our concepts of capitalization and grammar, the early church was big 'C' Catholic. *"For [Catholic] is the* **peculiar name of this Holy Church***, the mother of us all, which is the spouse of our Lord Jesus Christ, The Only-begotten Son of God"* (Cyril of Jerusalem, *The Catechetical Lectures*, §18.26, c. 347/8, **emphasis** added). So while this explanation does help us distinguish the term from the Catholic branch of the church, it does not truly account for the way in which the term is used by the church.

Given the difficulties, why can we not use another word? Attempts have been made to avoid the term. The most common attempt is to return to the common definition of the term 'universal.' However, this solution fails to appreciate the secondary connotation that developed alongside this 'dictionary' definition of the term. Whether we like it or not, it is part of the vocabulary of Christianity.

Why CTV Chooses to Keep It

We join our brothers and sisters across space and time in using the term 'catholic' to describe the church for the following reasons:

- ❖ It is a term rich in heritage completely separate of its misuse by the Roman Catholic Church.
- ❖ It is a time-tested term that still stands even after weathering a great deal of objection.
- ❖ It is a term without a precise substitute.
- ❖ It represents a rich concept that must not be ignored.

"The church is catholic. Catholic means to possess the whole truth, to stand continuous with the past and to reject the spirit of sectarianism. The full catholicity of the church is shown more in the totality of her life than in any particular cultural manifestation. Thus, we need to affirm our identity with the whole church, both past and present."[26]

---

[26] Robert Webber, *Common Roots*, 1978; Reprint (Zondervan, 2009), p.277

Appendix 4

LITURGY OF THE SACRED SERVICE

The Word of God

Preparation for the Word

- ❖ Welcome

- ☖ Lighting of the Candles

    As we light these candles we set aside the next few moments to worship our Almighty God. Saints of the Lord prepare your hearts to give praise to the Lord and listen to his Spirit speak to the church.

- ❖ Invocation

    Leader may freely pray, or may choose to use the prayer below:

    Almighty God, to you all hearts are open, all desires known, and from you no secrets are hid: Cleanse the thoughts of our hearts by the inspiration of your Holy Spirit, that we may perfectly love you, and worthily magnify your holy Name; through Christ our Lord. Amen.

- ❖ Psalm for the Day

- ♪ Hymns and Spiritual Songs

Proclamation of the Word

- ❖ Old Testament Lectionary Reading
    Reader: *This is the Word of God.*
    People: *The word of the Lord endures forever. Amen.*

❖ Gospel Lectionary Reading
Reader: *This is the Gospel of the Lord.*
People: *Lord Jesus, your words are spirit and life. Amen.*

❖ New Testament Epistle Lectionary Reading
Reader: *This is what the Spirit says to the churches.*
People: *Your word is a lamp to my feet and a light to my path. Amen.*

♬ The Chief Song

❖ Teaching of the Word

Response to the Word

❖ Prayers of the People

The Table of the Lord

The Creed, Confession, and the Peace (Preparation for the Table)

Celebrant and People Affirm the Nicene Creed

We believe in one God, the Father Almighty, maker of heaven and earth, of all things visible and invisible.

We believe in one Lord Jesus Christ, the only begotten Son of God, begotten of the Father before all ages, God from God, Light from Light, true God from true God, begotten, not created, of the same essence as the Father, Through whom all things were made.

Who for us men and for our salvation came down from heaven and was incarnate by the Holy Spirit and the Virgin Mary, and became human. Who for us too was crucified under Pontius Pilate, suffered and was buried. The third day he rose again according to the Scriptures, ascended into heaven and is seated at the right hand of the Father. He will come again in glory to judge the living and the dead, and his kingdom will have no end.

We believe in the Holy Spirit, the Lord and life-giver, who proceeds from the Father and the Son, who together with the Father and the Son is worshipped and glorified, who spoke by the prophets.

We believe in one holy catholic and apostolic church.

We acknowledge one baptism for the forgiveness of sin, and we look for the resurrection of the dead and the life of the age to come.

Amen.

Celebrant Says

Worthy are you, our Lord and God, to receive glory and honor and power forever.

All Pray

If, in the presence of your perfect holiness, we say we have no sin, we deceive ourselves, and the truth is not in us. If we confess our sins, you are faithful and just to forgive us our sins and to cleanse us from all unrighteousness.

(All Assume a Humble Posture of Bowing or Kneeling)

Celebrant Leads the Congregation in the Confession of Sin

[Celebrant may freely lead the community in the confession of sin, or may choose to use the liturgy to the right.]

[Liturgical Option for the Confession of Sin]
Celebrant Prays

Most merciful God, we confess that we have sinned against you in thought, word, and deed, by what we have done, and by what we have left undone. We have not loved you with our whole heart; we have not loved our neighbors as ourselves. We are truly sorry and we humbly repent, for the sake of your Son Jesus Christ, have mercy on us and forgive us; that we may delight in your will, and walk in your ways, to the glory of your Name.

And we respond together...

All Respond
Lord, have mercy on us.

(Moment of silence for personal confession)

Celebrant Says

> Gracious Father, you sent your Son to destroy the works of the devil. You made us alive together with him, having forgiven our sin, by canceling the record of debt that stood against us, nailing it to the cross. You disarmed the rulers and authorities and put them to open shame, by triumphing over them in Christ's death and resurrection. We now draw near to your throne with confidence, knowing that we will receive mercy and find grace. Amen.

Celebrant Stands and Says

> Greet one another in the love of Christ. And if you have anything against a brother or sister, reconcile with them. Christ himself is our peace.

Holy Communion (Reenactment of the Table)

Celebrant Stands and Exclaims (People Sit)

> Give thanks to the LORD, for he is good, for his steadfast love endures forever! Let everything that has breath praise the Lord!

[Everyone Sings a Song of Praise to the Lord]

Celebrant Declares the Story of God in Christ

> Eternal God our Lord you are the creator and ruler of all things. In pride, Satan rebelled against you and ignited a cosmic war.

All Say

> Though we were created in your own image, we joined the rebellion by obeying Satan, the ancient serpent. In our sin we were separated from you and fell under the power of the evil

one. Your creation was plunged into darkness and subjected to death.

Celebrant Says

Lord, in your infinite mercy, you promised to send a Savior to crush evil and redeem a people for yourself. In the fullness of time, you sent your own Son, Jesus, down from heaven to invade the dark realm of Satan. Through Christ's life, death, resurrection, and ascension, you defeated the devil and opened the kingdom of heaven to all believers.

All Say

Very soon, you will send your Son again to this world and he will completely conquer Satan and all demonic activity. He will destroy sin and death and establish your eternal kingdom.

Celebrant Blesses the Elements

As we celebrate this memorial of our redemption, Lord, we pray that in your goodness and mercy your Holy Spirit may descend upon us, and upon these gifts, the bread of life and the cup of salvation, the Body and Blood of your Son Jesus Christ.

Grant that all who share this bread and cup may become one body and one spirit, a living sacrifice in Christ, to the praise of your Name.

All Pray the Lord's Prayer

As our Savior taught us, we now pray,
Our Father in heaven,
Hallowed be your name;
Your kingdom come, Your will be done on earth as it is in heaven;
Give us this day our daily bread;

And forgive us our debts, as we also have forgiven our debtors;
And lead us not into temptation, but deliver us from evil;
For yours is the kingdom and the power and the glory forever.
Amen

Celebrant Taking the Bread and Breaking It Says

On the night before he died for us, our Lord Jesus Christ took bread; and when he had given thanks to you, he broke it, and gave it to his disciples, and said, "Take, eat: This is my Body, which is given for you. Do this for the remembrance of me."

(Pass the Bread as All Sing Communion Song Verse 1)

Celebrant Lifts the Bread and Says

The Body of Christ, the bread of heaven.

(The Church Partakes Together)

Celebrant Taking the Cup Says

After supper he took the cup; and when he had given thanks, he gave it to them, and said, "Drink this, all of you: This is my Blood of the new Covenant, which is shed for you and for many for the forgiveness of sins. Whenever you drink it, do this for the remembrance of me."

(Pass the Cup as All Sing Communion Song Verse 2)

Celebrant Lifts the Cup and Says

The Blood of Christ, the cup of salvation.

(The Church Partakes Together)

Celebrant Prays

> Eternal God, our Father, you have graciously accepted us as
> living members of your Son, our Savior Jesus Christ, and you
> have fed us with spiritual food in the Sacrament of his Body and
> Blood. Send us into the world in the power of your Holy Spirit to
> proclaim and demonstrate your gospel so those who live in
> darkness may turn to the light and from the power of Satan to
> God, that they may receive forgiveness of sins and a place
> among those who are sanctified by faith in Christ our Victor, the
> coming king who destroys the works of the devil.

All Say

> Come, Lord Jesus. Amen.

Response to the Table

♫   Closing Song

🕯   Extinguishing of the Candles

> *As we extinguish these candles, we are reminded that although*
> *these lights go out, we carry the light of Christ with us wherever*
> *we go this week. Saints of the Lord, prepare yourselves to fight the*
> *battle with strength and courage as we follow Christ our king.*

❖   Benediction

Appendix 5

LITURGY OF BAPTISM

If Baptism is celebrated as a part of the Sacred Service, this liturgy should follow the teaching of the Word.

Presentation

Celebrant Says

> Today, we have the joy of celebrating the baptism of [*Name(s)*]. The sacrament of baptism is our incorporation into the visible body of Christ. It is a public pledge to renounce sin and evil, to die to ourselves, and to live under the lordship of Jesus Christ as a part of his church.

[The Celebrant turns to the Candidate(s) and asks]

> Do you desire to be baptized? If so respond, "I do."

Candidate(s) Answers

> I do.

Examination: Renouncing the Devil, the World, and the Flesh, and Turning to Christ[27]

Celebrant Asks the Following Questions and the Candidate(s) Responds with the Answers

> *Question:* Do you renounce Satan, the dominion of darkness, and all the spiritual forces of evil that rebel and war against God? If so, respond 'I renounce them.'
>
> *Answer:* I renounce them.

---

[27] An alternate form of the Examination is provided at the end of the Baptismal Liturgy especially to be used with younger candidates.

Question: Do you renounce the evil powers of this world which corrupt and destroy the creatures of God? If so, respond 'I renounce them.'

Answer: I renounce them.

Question: Do you renounce all the sinful desires of your flesh that entice you away from loving and obeying God? If so, respond 'I renounce them.'

Answer: I renounce them.

Question: Do you trust Jesus Christ as your Savior, put your faith completely in him, and promise to obey his commands? If so, respond 'Jesus is Lord.'

Answer: Jesus is Lord.

Baptismal Vows

Celebrant Says

[*Name(s)*] have been delivered from the dominion of darkness, and transferred into the kingdom of the Son. Let us all join with them now and renew our own baptismal vows.

Celebrant Asks the Following Questions and the Congregation of Baptized Christians Joins the Candidate(s) in Responding with the Answers

Question: Do you join with the church in believing and affirming the scriptural witness to the person and work of God the Father, the Son, and the Holy Spirit, summarized by the Creed, and will you remain faithful to the teachings of the apostles and the prophets? If so, respond 'I believe the Truth.'

Answer: I believe the Truth.

Question: Will you share with the church in worshipping the true and living God, as a member of the royal priesthood, and will you live always for the glory of God alone? If so, respond 'I will worship the King.'

Answer: I will worship the King.

Question: Will you daily take up your cross with the church and follow the Lord Jesus, being conformed to his image by the Holy Spirit, resisting sin and evil, and disciplining yourself for godliness by the grace that God supplies? If so, respond 'I will follow Jesus, the Nazarene.'

Answer: I will follow Jesus, the Nazarene.

Question: Will you enlist with the church and put on the full armor of God so that you may carry out the mission of Jesus to advance God's kingdom in the world and to destroy the works of the devil? If so, respond 'I will serve the Lord.'

Answer: I will serve the Lord.

Prayer

Celebrant Prays

Let us pray together.

We thank you Father for the water of baptism, in which you make us one with Christ in his death and burial, in order that we may be one with him in his victory over sin and death and his new life. You adopt us into your family, the body of Christ, you ordain us into your royal priesthood that worships and serves you and you enlist us as part of your spiritual army.

Sanctify this water by the power of your Holy Spirit, and grant that all who are baptized into the death of Jesus Christ your Son may live in the power of his resurrection and look for him to come again in glory; who lives and reigns now and forever. Amen.

Holy Baptism

Celebrant Lay a Hand on the Back of the Candidate and Says

[Name] I baptize you in the name of the Father, and of the Son, and of the Holy Spirit.

Your old self is dead and buried with Christ.

[*Celebrant immerses the Candidate in the water, then brings them up and says*]

You are raised in Christ, a new creation.

[*Celebrant repeats this for each Candidate*]

Celebrant Says

The family of God is invited to come and lay hands on our [brother(s)/sister(s)] as we pray for [him/her/them].

[*Celebrant allows time for the congregation to pray over the newly baptized and closes with the following prayer*]

Heavenly Father, we thank you that by water and the Holy Spirit, you have poured your grace and love upon [Name(s)] and upon us all. We rejoice with you as you embrace [him/her/them] into your family, and humbly ask that you sustain [him/her/them] to the end. Amen.

Celebrant Says to Each Newly Baptized Person

[Name] you are sealed by the Holy Spirit and marked as Christ's own forever.

The Service proceeds with the Prayers of the People

An Alternate form of the Examination: Renouncing the Devil, the World, and the Flesh, and Turning to Christ

Celebrant Asks the Following Questions and the Candidate(s) Responds with the Answers

Question: Do you say no to Satan, and his kingdom of evil spiritual forces that battle against God? If so, respond 'I do.'

Answer: I do.

Question: Do you say no to the world and all the bad things around you that go against God's kingdom? If so, respond 'I do.'

Answer: I do.

Question: Do you say not to all the sinful desires of your flesh that take you away from loving and obeying God? If so, respond 'I do.'

Answer: I do.

Question: Do you trust Jesus Christ as your Savior, put your faith completely in him, and promise to obey his commands? If so, respond 'Jesus is Lord.'

Answer: Jesus is Lord.

Service Continues with the Baptismal Vows

Appendix 6

OTHER CTV SERVICE HELPS

Baby Dedication

❖ Parent(s)' Commitment to Raise the Child(ren) to Follow Christ

❖ Reading of a Select Scripture for the Child(ren)

❖ Prayer of Thanksgiving and Blessing for the Child(ren)

Sample Outline for Healing

(Adapted from *The Book of Common Prayer*)

❖ Reading of James 5.14–16

❖ Person needing healing comes forward.

❖ The church lays hands on him/her.

❖ The church prays for the Lord's healing in the person's body and spirit.

❖ The minister anoints the person with oil by making the shape of a cross on his/her forehead.

❖ The minister prays that as the person is anointed with oil on the outside, the Lord would anoint the person with his healing presence to forgive sin, drive away suffering, and bring restoration.

Sample Outline for Intercessory Prayer

Could be used in cases where restoration, breakthrough, protection, freedom, provision, or other needs are present.

- ❖ The person in need comes forward.

- ❖ The church lays hands on him/her.

- ❖ The minister reads a portion of Scripture appropriate to the need. Suggested Readings:

  - ⇨ Restoration – 1 John 1.7–9

  - ⇨ Breakthrough – 2 Timothy 1.7

  - ⇨ Protection – Psalm 3, Psalm 27

  - ⇨ Freedom – Galatians 5.1

  - ⇨ Provision – Philippians 4.6–7, 19

- ❖ Others in the church pray for the person in need.

- ❖ The minister closes by reading Ephesians 3.20–21, 2 Thessalonians 3.16–18, or Jude 24–25.

Appendix 7

Understanding the Church Year – A Guide to Colors, Themes, & History

Understanding the Seasons

The seasons and observances follow the outline of the life and ministry of Jesus allowing us to tread in his footsteps year after year.

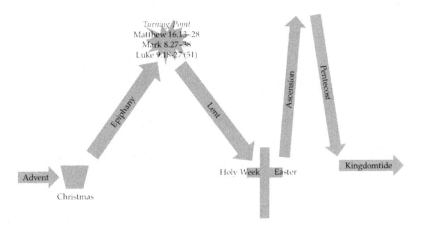

Advent – *The Anticipation of Christ*

Name: Latin for 'Coming' or 'Arrival'

Emphasis: We recall the days prior to the first coming of Christ and repent as we look forward to his second coming.

Colors: Purple – Royalty, Repentance (Weeks 1, 2, 4); Pink – Joy, Happiness (Week 3)

Christmas – *The Birth of Christ*

Name: Originally 'The Christ Mass', or the service celebrating incarnation of Christ (the term Mass is from the Old English for 'dismissal' and was likely the final word of the church service)

Emphasis: We celebrate that God the Son became flesh by the Holy Spirit and the virgin Mary and dwelt among us.

Color: Gold – Light, The Majesty and Glory of God's Presence

Epiphany – *The Manifestation of Christ*

Name: Greek for 'Manifestation'

Emphasis: We affirm that in Jesus of Nazareth the kingdom of God is shining its light into the dark realm of the devil.

Colors: Green – Hope, Life; Gold – Light, The Majesty and Glory of God's Presence (The Epiphany, Transfiguration Sunday)

Lent – *The Lowliness of Christ*

Name: Short for Lenten, from the Old English for 'Springtime'

Emphasis: We take up the cross and walk with Christ the path of complete humility and servanthood.

Colors: Purple – Royalty, Repentance

Holy Week – *The Suffering and Death of Christ*

Name: Traditionally the final three days are called the *Paschal Triduum*, which means the three days related to our Passover.

Emphasis: We share in the sufferings and death of Christ in order that we may be raised to new life in him.

Colors: Purple – Royalty, Repentance; Black – Mourning, Death (Good Friday, Holy Saturday)

Easter – *The Resurrection of Christ*

> *Name:* Historically called *Pascha* from the Greek for Passover; Easter was adapted from the name of an ancient English month equivalent to April.

> *Emphasis:* We shout for joy because Jesus is risen from the dead and seated at the right hand of the Father; Christ is the victor over sin, death, and Satan!

> *Colors:* Gold – Light, The Majesty and Glory of God's Presence

Pentecost – *The Coming of the Holy Spirit*

> *Name:* From the Greek for '50'; the Holy Spirit arrived 50 days after the resurrection.

> *Emphasis:* We remember that the arrival of Holy Spirit on the church means new life and amazing power to declare and demonstrate the victory of Christ to the ends of the earth.

> *Colors:* Red – Holy Spirit as a Fire

Kingdomtide (Ordinary Time) *–A Season of Christ's Headship, Harvest, and Hope*

> *Name:* The suffix 'tide' is Old English for a period of time. Kingdomtide then is the time of the advance of the kingdom. Ordinary means numbered (as in ordinal numbers 1st, 2nd, 3rd, etc.)

> *Emphasis:* In these last days the Spirit-filled church submits to the headship of Christ our Lord, labors for the harvest of Christ our Savior, and prepares the way for the second coming of Christ our King.

Colors: Gold – Light, The Majesty and Glory of God's Presence (Trinity Sunday, Reign of Christ the King); Green – Hope, Life; Red – Blood of the Martyrs (All Saints' Day)

Understanding the Calendar

1. The Date of Easter – The First Council of Nicaea (325) established the date of Easter as the first Sunday after the full moon following the northern hemisphere's vernal equinox. This Sunday always falls between 3/22–4/25.

2. Dependent Celebrations – A 90-day Moving Block

    a. Ash Wednesday – 40 Days Before Easter

    b. Ascension Day – 40 Days After Easter, but is usually celebrated the Sunday before Pentecost (6th Sunday of Easter)

    c. Pentecost – 50 Days After Easter (7th Sunday of Easter)

3. Epiphany and Kingdomtide adjust on either side to compensate.

    a. Weeks 6–8 of Epiphany = Propers 1–3 of Kingdomtide

    b. Epiphany can be as short as 5 Sundays, or as long as 9. The last Sunday always celebrates the Transfiguration of Christ.

    c. Kingdomtide can begin anywhere between Propers 1–9. The first Sunday of Kingdomtide is always Trinity Sunday.

Understanding the History and Development of the Church Year

1. The Jewish Liturgical Calendar

    a. The church year has its roots in the Jewish festival calendar laid out by the Lord in the Old Testament.

    b. The Lord designed for his people, Israel, a program of shared spiritual formation that included regular observances, festivals, feasts, and fasts.

    c. Sabbath – The Foundation of the Calendar

        i. Weekly Saturday Rest – 7 Day Cycle

        ii. Sabbatical Year Rest – 7 Year Cycle

        iii. Year of Jubilee – 7x7 Year Cycle

    d. Major Seasonal Observances (see Leviticus 23)

        i. Feast of Passover/Unleavened Bread (Mid-April) – Re-enactment of the night before the great Exodus; all males required to appear in Jerusalem.

        ii. Feast of Pentecost/Weeks/First-fruits (7 Weeks after Passover, Early June)– Celebration of the first-fruits of the harvest, and remembers the giving of the Law at Sinai; all males required to appear in Jerusalem.

        iii. Feast of Trumpets (Early October) – Civil New Year [*Rosh Hashanah*]

        iv. The Day of Atonement [Yom Kippur] (Mid-October) – High holy day of the Israelite year; a solemn fast, and day of repentance, where the high priest enters into the Holy of Holies and cleanses both the nation and the temple from sin.

v. Feast of Tabernacles (Late October) – Marks the completion of the harvest, and remembers the wandering of Israel in the desert; all males required to appear in Jerusalem.

e. Seasonal Observances Added Later

i. Festival of Purim (Mid-March) – Originates in the mid 400's B.C. It celebrates the deliverance of the Jews narrated in the book of Esther.

ii. Festival of Lights [*Hanukkah*] (Late December) – Originated in 164 B.C.; Celebrates the rededication of the Temple beginning the brief period where the Jewish Maccabees ruled in Judea.

2. Early Jewish Christianity

a. The earliest Christians thought of themselves as essentially Jewish (see Acts 2.46, 3.1, 5.20,42, 11.26 [It is not until here that a new name, 'Christian,' is used to describe them.])

b. The Jewish festival calendar centered on two foci – The Exodus and the harvest.

c. Building on the God-ordained festival calendar, the early church began to reshape the liturgical year in light of the coming of the prophesied Messiah, who brought the new Exodus, and who calls us into a new harvest.

d. Saturday Sabbath → Sunday, The Lord's Day (in honor of the day of Christ's resurrection; see Acts 20.7, 1 Corinthians 16.2, Revelation 1.10)

e. Passover → Easter (1 Corinthians 5.7–8)

f. Pentecost, Festival of First-fruits of the Wheat Harvest → Pentecost the Celebration of the coming of the Holy Spirit bringing in the First-fruits of the great Spiritual Harvest

3. The Development of the Church Year

a. The weekly Sunday celebration (centering on hearing the Word, and taking communion) and the yearly celebration of Easter in place of Passover have legitimate claim to originating in the time of the biblical Apostles.

b. Pentecost is celebrated with a distinct Christian emphasis in the earliest post-Apostolic time, likely the 100's. This development constitutes the first season of the church year, the 50 days of the Easter season.

c. The other major seasons are added over the next 200 years.

    i. Advent – A period of preparation for the nativity of Christ is in place by the mid-300's. The length of this time, however, varied from 3 weeks to 40 days until the 500's when Gregory the Great fixed it at 4 weeks.

    ii. Christmas & Epiphany – These two celebrations are closely linked. Originally, Easter celebrated "the entire mystery of Christ including the incarnation with the moment of conception, which put the nativity nine months later" (Cobb,

467). These seasons were likely united in their origin. The first clear reference to these as yearly celebrations of the church comes in 361. The ancient festival celebrated the nativity, the visit of the Magi, the baptism, and the first miracle of Jesus (the Miracle at Cana). Christmas likely becomes independent of Epiphany in the early 300's.

iii. Lent – The first mention of Lent is at the Council of Nicaea (325), although it is widely known and accepted by then. This likely puts its origin in the 200's.

iv. Holy Week – Palm Sunday was reenacted yearly in Jerusalem as early as the 300's, and was imitated in other places starting in the 400's. The Paschal Triduum originated around this same time.

d. Other observances are added by the church as the centuries passed.

i. All Saints' Day – As early as the 400's Christians celebrated a day honoring the martyrs of the church. In 609/10, the church made All Saints' Day an official celebration of the church year.

ii. Trinity Sunday – Originates as a grassroots celebration in the 1000's, and is officially mandated as part of the church year in the 1300's.

iii. Christ the King – Instituted in 1925 to combat nationalism following World War I. Many Christians were displaying a loyalty to countries and leaders that eclipsed their loyalty to Christ and his church.

Note: Other forms of the church year include celebrations for various people and events on almost every day of the year.

e. Lectionaries developed alongside the church year as a schedule of appropriate readings for the days and seasons.

    i. Jewish tradition actually suggests that readings were associated with certain festivals and days in the time of Moses.

    ii. Whether this tradition is true or not, it is clear that lectionaries existed in Judaism during the second temple period (516 B.C.E. – A.D. 70). The Christian use of lectionaries seems to have been inherited from Judaism.

Appendix 8

RETRIEVING THE GREAT TRADITION

The Ancient Faith

Jude wrote his epistle to challenge the church "to contend for the faith that was once for all delivered to the saints" (Jude 3). Christianity neither began with us, nor is it fundamentally defined by us. We are in the position of receiving and embodying a faith that was defined in the ancient past. When we enter the body of Christ, we step into a river that has been flowing from the days of Christ, the apostles, and the prophets. We have only to embrace and contend for the ancient faith in an ever changing world.

An Urban Movement

As we seek an urban church planting movement, we see tremendous value in centering churches on what has been believed and practiced everywhere, always, by all Christians. The reproductive nature of a church planting movement demands that we answer the question, 'Is CTV reproducible?' The ability to reproduce means that CTV churches cannot be required to reinvent church with every new church plant. Certain beliefs, practices, and protocols need to be standardized. But as soon as we start talking about standardizing things, we must answer a second question, 'What is worth reproducing everywhere?' CTV wants to build into its DNA that which is most truly and uniquely Christian. Reproduction happens after a kind. Children inevitably look and act like their parents. The same is true of churches. We want the bloodline of CTV churches to bear the indelible mark of the faith once for all delivered to the saints.

Christ the Victor, therefore, intentionally seeks to retrieve the Great Tradition in our theology, worship, spirituality, and mission. "The

Great Tradition represents that central core of Christian belief and practice derived from the Scriptures that runs between the time of Christ and the middle of the fifth century. In a formative way, this Tradition articulates the Church's faith and practice, its joyful, faithful response to the truth of God's sovereign work of grace in the world" (Davis, *Sacred Roots*, 74).

Appendix 9

RECOMMENDED BIBLIOGRAPHY

Please note: CTV does not endorse every idea in these texts. We recommend these as helpful resources, but with every book "test everything; hold fast to what is good" (1 Thess 5.21). Those marked with a ⇨ are regarded as particularly helpful.

The Urban Poor

❖ Roger Greenway and Timothy Monsma, *Cities: Missions' New Frontier*, 2nd Ed., Baker Books, 2000.

⇨ Keith Philips, *Out of Ashes*, World Impact Press, 1996.

The Ancient Faith

❖ Don Allsman, *Jesus Cropped from the Picture*, The Urban Ministry Institute, 2009.

❖ David Bercot, ed. *A Dictionary of Early Christian Beliefs*, Hendrickson, 1998.

⇨ Don Davis, *Sacred Roots*, The Urban Ministry Institute, 2010.

❖ Thomas Oden, *Classical Christianity: A Systematic Theology*, Harper One, 2009.

Christus Victor

❖ Gustaf Aulen, *Christus Victor*, trans. A.G. Hebert WIPF & Stock, 2003 (orig. Macmilllan, 1961).

⇨ Robert Webber, *Ancient-Future Faith*, Baker Academic, 1999.

❖ Robert Webber, *The Majestic Tapestry*, Thomas Nelson, 1986 (out of print).

The Nicene Creed

⇨ Ronald Heine, *Classical Christian Doctrine*, Baker Academic, 2013.

❖ Christopher Seitz, *Nicene Christianity*, Brazos Press, 2004.

Liturgy and Worship

❖ Chelsyn Jones, Geoffrey Wainwright, et al, eds., *The Study of Liturgy*, SPCK & Oxford Press, 1992.

❖ Frank Senn, *Introduction to Liturgy*, Fortress Press, 2012.

⇨ Robert Webber, *Ancient-Future Worship*, Baker Academic, 2008.

❖ Robert Webber, *Common Roots*, Zondervan, 2009 reprint (orig. 1978).

The Church Year

❖ Anne Field, *Delivered from Evil*, Servant Books, 2005.

⇨ Bobby Gross, *Living the Christian Year*, IVP, 2009.

❖ Robert Webber, *Ancient-Future Time*, Baker Books, 2004.

Church Planting Movements

⇨ David Garrison, *Church Planting Movements*, Wigtake Resources, 2003. (Also available in an abbreviated booklet form; PDF may be downloaded for free at www.churchplantingmovements.com)

❖ Robert Webber, *Ancient-Future Evangelism*, Baker Books, 2003.

Prayer, Healing, and Deliverance

⇨ Paul Billheimer, *Destined for the Throne*, Bethany House, 2005 (orig 1979).

❖ Jack Deere, *Surprised by the Power of God*, Zondervan, 1996.

❖ Don Williams, *Signs, Wonders, and the Kingdom of God*, Sunrise Reprints, 1989, 2011.

❖ John Wimber, *Power Healing*, Harper One, 2009 reprint.

Women in Ministry

❖ Gilbert Bilezikian, *Beyond Sex Roles: What the Bible Says about a Woman's Place in Church and Family*, 3rd Ed., Baker, 2006.

❖ Philip Barton Payne, *Man and Woman, One in Christ: An Exegetical and Theological Study of Paul's Letter*, Zondervan, 2009.

⇨ Ronald W. Pierce and Rebecca Merrill Groothius eds., *Discovering Biblical Equality*, IVP, 2005.

Understanding the Bible

❖ Gordon Fee and Douglas Stuart, *How to Read the Bible for All Its Worth*, 2nd Ed., Zondervan, 2009.

⇨ Norm Geisler, *To Understand the Bible Look for Jesus*, WIPF & Stock, 2002 (orig. Baker, 1979).

❖ Robert Webber, *Who Gets to Narrate the World*, IVP, 2008.

Appendix 10

CONTACT AND RESOURCES

Contact Us:

❖ By Email: ctvchurch@worldimpact.org

❖ Or By Mail:
3701 E 13th St.
Wichita, KS 67208
Attn: Christ the Victor

For More Information Visit: www.ctvchurch.org

Other CTV Resources (available at Amazon.com; links on CTV website):

Christ the Victor Church: A Quick Guide

The *Quick Guide* contains the second section of this book (pp. 11–25). It is a brief summary of CTV's common identity and shared practices.

Christ the Victor Church: The Guidebook

The *Guidebook* is a thorough and in depth summary of CTV's common identity and shared practices.

Recommended TUMI Resources (www.tumi.org)

❖ Chronological Bible Reading Guide

❖ Church Year Calendar

❖ *Once Upon A Time: The Cosmic Drama through a Biblical Narration of the World*

❖ *Let God Arise! Prayer Guide*